CLASSIC COUNTRY FURNITURE

ROBERT BELKE

POPULAR WOODWORKING BOOKS
CINCINNATI, OHIO
www.popularwoodworking.com

READ THIS IMPORTANT SAFETY NOTICE

To prevent accidents, keep safety in mind while you work. Use the safety guards installed on power equipment; they are for your protection. When working on power equipment, keep fingers away from saw blades, wear safety goggles to prevent injuries from flying wood chips and sawdust, wear headphones to protect your hearing, and consider installing a dust vacuum to reduce the amount of airborne sawdust in your woodshop. Don't wear loose clothing, such as neckties or shirts with loose sleeves, or jewelry, such as rings, necklaces or bracelets, when working on power equipment. Tie back long hair to prevent it from getting caught in your equipment. People who are sensitive to certain chemicals should check the chemical content of any product before using it. The author and editors who compiled this book have tried to make the contents as accurate and correct as possible. Plans, illustrations, photographs and text have been carefully checked. All instructions, plans and projects should be carefully read, studied and understood before beginning construction. Due to the variability of local conditions, construction materials, skill levels, etc., neither the author nor Popular Woodworking Books assumes any responsibility for any accidents, injuries, damages or other losses incurred resulting from the material presented in this book.

METRIC CONVERSION CHART

TO CONVERT	TO	MULTIPLY BY
Inches	Centimeters	2.54
Centimeters	Inches	0.4
Feet	Centimeters	30.5
Centimeters	Feet	0.03
Yards	Meters	0.9
Meters	Yards	1.1
Sq. Inches	Sq. Centimeters	6.45
Sq. Centimeters	Sq. Inches	0.16
Sq. Feet	Sq. Meters	0.09
Sq. Meters	Sq. Feet	10.8
Sq. Yards	Sq. Meters	0.8
Sq. Meters	Sq. Yards	1.2
Pounds	Kilograms	0.45
Kilograms	Pounds	2.2
Ounces	Grams	28.4
Grams	Ounces	0.04

Classic Country Furniture. Copyright © 1999 by Robert E. Belke. Manufactured in China . All rights reserved. No part of this book may be reproduced in any form or by any electronic or mechanical means including information storage and retrieval systems without permission in writing from the publisher, except by a reviewer, who may quote brief passages in a review. Published by Popular Woodworking Books, an imprint of F&W Publications, Inc., 1507 Dana Avenue, Cincinnati, Ohio, 45207. First edition.

Visit our Web site at www.popularwoodworking.com for information on more resources for woodworkers.

Other fine Popular Woodworking Books are available from your local bookstore or direct from the publisher.

03   02   01   00   99   5   4   3   2   1

Library of Congress Cataloging-in-Publication Data

Belke, Robert E.
     Classic country furniture / by Robert Belke.
          p.   cm.
     Includes index.
     ISBN 1-55870-544-9 (alk. paper)
     1. Furniture making.   2. Country furniture.   I. Title.
TT194.B453   2000   99-049563
684.1'04—dc21   CIP

Edited by Michael Berger
Cover designed by Brian Roeth
Interior production by Kathy Gardner
Production coordinated by Sara Dumford
Computer illustrations by Len Churchill

About the Author

Robert E. Belke has been a custom furniture builder for many years, working in the styles of Shaker, Early American and Arts and Crafts. His last book, *Arts and Crafts Woodworking Projects,* was published by Stackpole Publishing in 1998.

Robert is married, served with the United States Navy and is the father of six grown children. A graduate of Syracuse University, he currently lives in Liverpool, New York.

Acknowledgments

Special thanks to Robert Becker for his advice and encouragement in writing this book. I would also like to thank Tim Rinehart of Woodcraft for the numerous suggestions and helpful hints he gave me for many projects in this book.

Dedication

To my wife, Carol, for her patience and encouragement.

Table of Contents

CREAM CAN LAMP • page 14

CANDLE STICKS • page 18

NESTED TABLES • page 36

SPIRAL STAIRCASE TABLE • page 42

WALL CABINET • page 50

DRAWER BOOKCASE • page 64

WALL SCONCES • page 108

TRESTLE TABLE • page 70

SMALL DRAWER TABLE • page 102

INDOOR-OUTDOOR TABLE • page 122

Introduction

The term "country furniture" means different things to different people. To some, it brings to mind the simplicity and serviceability reminiscent of early pioneer furniture. To others, the functional utility and beauty of Pennsylvania Dutch, Early American and Shaker creations. Being the melting pot that it is, America has enjoyed the influx of many styles of furniture to our shores, including, but not limited to, Chippendale, Shaker, Victorian, and Arts and Crafts furniture. Many of the techniques used to fabricate these styles have also found their way into the American country furniture.

The projects I have assembled in this book are fun to build and should give you a measure of pride and satisfaction from working with wood and creating something of your own. Although I describe the use of machine tools in making each of the articles, there is nothing stopping you from using hand tools instead of the table saw or the jointer/planer. Don't forget that all the farmer or miller had to use, many years ago, were the very basic hand tools.

A number of projects also require you to use a wood lathe. Not only can you create beautiful items on this machine, it's a fun tool to use as well. There are a number of good wood lathes on the market, and they can be found in the various woodworking stores or in a number of woodworking catalogs.

Some projects need such things as doweled joints or tapered legs. In Tools and Techniques, you'll find designs for some simple yet effective jigs that should aid you in making these joints and cuts.

The woods used for the projects, such as cherry, oak and walnut, are all native to the United States, and are excellent woods to use in the construction of furniture. However, if you have access to other woods, such as butternut, sycamore, pear or pine, you can create your masterpiece using those choices instead.

Tools and Techniques

I made all the projects shown in this book using woodworking machines, such as a table saw, a router, a drill press and a lathe. This isn't to say that hand tools, such as saws, planes and braces and bits, can't be used to build any project in the book. It will just take a little longer to complete each operation. The projects will turn out just as beautiful. Some people get great satisfaction using the simpler hand tools.

Recommended Tools

Some of the tools recommended for the construction of the projects in this book are as follows:

- a table saw, similar to the 10" Delta 34-444 contractor's saw
- a floor or bench-mounted drill press, similar to a Delta 11-990, the Ryobi 1850 or the Sears 21313N
- a band saw, similar to the Delta 28-275, the Jet JWBS-14CS, the Ryobi BS900 or the Sears 24835N
- a 6" jointer/planer similar to the Grizzly G1182 or the Delta 37-90
- a 12" thickness planer similar to the Ryobi AP12K, the Grizzly G1017 or the DeWALT DW733K
- a router similar to the Bosch 1613EVS, the Ryobi R180 or the DeWALT DW621
- a belt sander similar to a 3"×21" Porter Cable 352VS, the DeWALT DW431 or the Bosch 127DVS
- a 5" random orbit sander similar to the Porter Cable 333P, the DeWALT DW423K or the Ryobi RS200.
- a finishing sander similar to the Porter Cable 330P or the Ryobi S605D
- a Ryobi DBJ59 detail biscuit joiner
- pipe clamps
- various tape measures, rulers, dowel centers, calipers, squares, pencils, yellow and water-resistant glues

A Simple Doweling Jig

This jig, used in conjunction with dowel centers, enables you to properly locate the positions of connecting dowels, thereby assuring secure attachment of table legs to their aprons. Initially, dowel holes can be bored either in the leg or in the apron (it doesn't matter which). The dowel centers are placed in holes, and the apron is then pressed into the leg. Bore the matching holes based on the marks made.

To make the jig, cut out the parts as listed in the materials list. The brace is cut to a 45° angle. Drill and screw together the back to the brace, and then attach the base. Glue on the guide, making sure it's at 90° to the base (see figures 1 and 2).

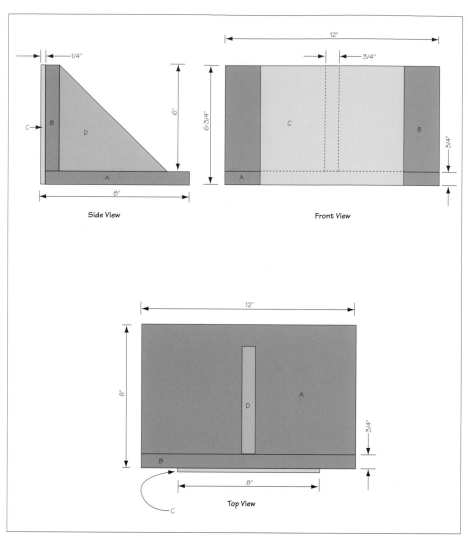

Side View   Front View   Top View

1 Typical dimensions for a doweling jig.

Doweling Jig Materials List

REF.	QTY	DIMENSIONS (IN INCHES)
A	1	¾ × 8 × 12
B	1	¾ × 6 × 12
C	1	¼ × 6 ¾ × 8
D	2	¾ × 6 × 6

All parts are birch plywood

2 By using the doweling jig, you can assure your dowel holes always mate up perfectly.

Circle-Routing Jig

This jig is used with a router to rout a clean outer edge for projects, such as the small dining table and the candle stand described later in this book. This design is just a suggestion—how the actual jig turns out depends upon the make of the particular router in use (see figures 3 & 4).

Lathe-Sizing Jig

Use this jig to quickly check the diameters of spindles you turn on a lathe without removing them. To make the jig, cut a 1¾" × 10⅛" piece of ¼" thick plywood. Bore ten holes as shown in the drawing with the same Forstner bits you'll use when constructing your projects (this will insure a good fit between parts). Then with a band saw, remove the waste. The holes can be used as fit checks for the spindle ends, while the half circles will check an in-process dimension while turning the part (see figures 5 and 6).

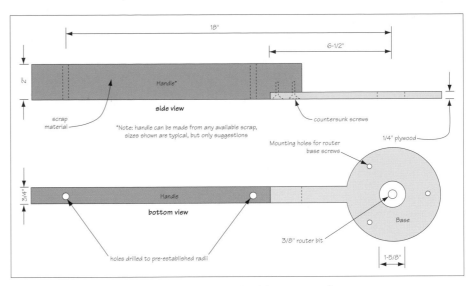

3 Dimensions for a typical circle-routing jig. Models vary greatly, so build yours to best work with your brand of router.

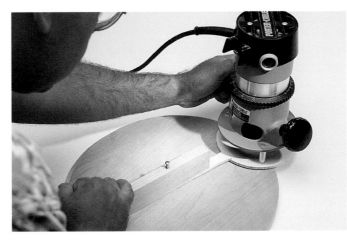

4 The circle-routing jig enables you to rout a clean, precise edge to any circular workpiece.

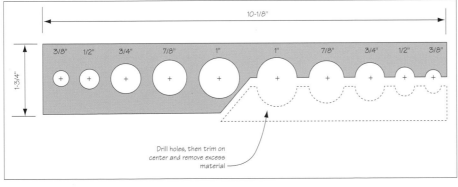

5 Typical dimensions for a spindle-sizing jig.

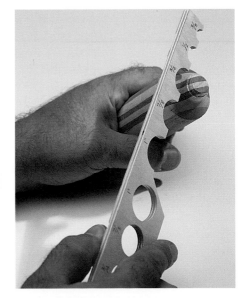

6 The spindle-sizing jig lets you quickly check common diameters without having to use either a caliper or a ruler.

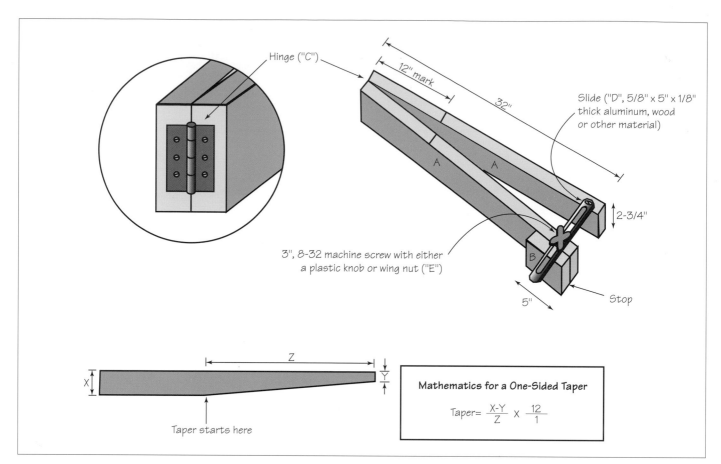

Hinge ("C")

12" mark

32"

Slide ("D", 5/8" x 5" x 1/8" thick aluminum, wood or other material)

A   A

2-3/4"

3", 8-32 machine screw with either a plastic knob or wing nut ("E")

B

Stop

5"

Z

X

Y

Taper starts here

Mathematics for a One-Sided Taper

$$Taper = \frac{X-Y}{Z} \times \frac{12}{1}$$

7 Mount the false top and shelves into the rabbet and dadoes. Use screws to reinforce the mounting.

A Simple Tapering Jig

Forbidding as they look, tapered legs are not that difficult to make, if you use a jig. Most woodworking catalogs sell tapering jigs, but you can save money by making your own.

To make this jig, cut the two arms to the dimensions listed in the materials list. Glue the stop to one of the arms. Holding the arms together, measure off and make a mark 12" from the end, and then screw a hinge to that same end. Cut a slot in the ⅛" aluminum, and drill a hole into the arm large enough to accept an 8-32 × 3" machine screw. Mount the slotted aluminum plate on the opposite arm, insert the 3" screw and screw on the wing nut (see figures 7 and 8).

The taper for any particular leg is calculated using the relationship shown in figure 7. Simply plug in the dimensions for X, Y and Z, make the calculation and multiply by 12. The distance

Tapering Jig Materials List

REF.	QTY	DIMENSIONS (IN INCHES)
A	2	¾ x 2¾ x 32
B	1	¾ x 2¾ x 5
C	1	Hinge to fit ends
D	1	⅝ x 5 x ⅛-thick aluminum
E	1	8-32 x 3 machine screw with wing nut

between the 12" marks can be set with a dial vernier caliper, such as a Stanley #35-019, or a ruler can be used to get an approximation. Set the distance between marks and tighten the wing nut.

To use the jig, place the tapering jig against the table saw fence and set the saw blade at a distance of X from the "Taper starts here" mark. Place the leg blank against the jig and slide the jig toward the saw blade, continuing until the taper is cut. Rotate the leg blank 90° and cut the second taper.

8 Tapering jigs can vary greatly in material and individual design. Here's one that uses a wooden slide rather than aluminum.

Common Woodworking Terms

BEVEL A cut that is not 90 degrees to a board's face, or the facet left by such a cut.

BISCUIT A thin, flat oval of compressed beech that is inserted between two pieces of wood into mating saw kerfs made by a biscuit or plate joining machine.

BRIDLE JOINT A joint that combines features of both lap joints and mortise and tenon. It has a U-shaped mortise in the end of the board.

BUTT JOINT Two flat facets of mating parts that fit flush together with no interlocking joinery.

CARPENTER'S GLUE White and yellow adhesives formulated for use with wood.

CASING The trim framing a window, door, or other opening.

CHALK LINE Line made by snapping a chalk-coated string against a plane.

CHECK A crack in wood material caused by drying, either just in the surface or in the ends of the board so the fibers have separated.

COMPOUND MITER A cut where the blade path is not perpendicular to the wood's end or edge and the blade tilt is not 90 degrees to the face.

COPING Sawing a negative profile in one piece to fit the positive profile of another, usually in molding.

COUNTERBORE A straight-sided drilled hole that recesses a screw head below the wood surface so a wood plug can cover it, or the bit which makes this hole.

COUNTERSINK A cone-shaped drilled hole whose slope angle matches the underside of a flat screw head and sinks it flush with the wood surface, or the tool which makes this hole.

CROSSCUT To saw wood perpendicular to the grain.

CUPPING A drying defect where one side of the board shrinks more across the grain than the other, causing the board to curl in on itself like a trough.

DADO A flat-bottomed, U-shaped milling cut of varying widths and depths but always running across the grain.

DOVETAIL JOINT A traditional joint characterized by interlocking fingers and pockets shaped like its name. It has exceptional resistance to tension.

DOWEL A small cylinder of wood that is used to reinforce a wood joint.

DRESSING The process of turning rough lumber into a smooth board with flat, parallel faces and straight, parallel edges and whose edges are square to the face.

EDGE LAP A notch into the edge of a board halfway across its width which forms half of an edge lap joint.

FINGERLAP A specific joint of the lap family which has straight, interwoven fingers; also called a box joint.

FINISH Varnish, stain, paint, or any mixture that protects a surface.

FLATSAWN The most common cut of lumber where the growth rings run predominantly across the end of the board; or its characteristic grain pattern.

FLUSH Level with an adjoining surface.

GRAIN PATTERN The visual appearance of wood grain. Types of grain pattern include flat, straight, curly, quilted, rowed, mottled, crotch, cathedral, beeswing, or bird's-eye.

HARDWOOD Wood from broadleaf deciduous trees, no matter what the density (balsa is a hardwood).

HEARTWOOD Wood from the core of a tree, usually darker and harder than newer wood.

JIG A shopmade or aftermarket device that assists in positioning and steadying the wood or tools.

JOINTING The process of making a board face straight and flat or an edge straight, whether by hand or machine.

KERF The visible path of subtracted wood left by a sawblade.

KEY An inserted joint-locking device, usually made of wood.

KNOCKDOWN JOINT A joint which is assembled without glue an can be disassembled and reassembled if necessary.

LAP JOINT A type of joint made by removing half the thickness or width of the parts and lapping them over each other.

LENGTH JOINT A joint which makes one longer wood unit out of two shorter ones by joining them end to end.

LEVEL Absolutely horizontal.

MILLING The process of removing material to leave a desired positive or negative profile in the wood.

MITER A generic term meaning mainly an angled cut across the face grain, or specifically 45 degree cut across the face, end grain, or along the grain. See also bevel.

MORTISE The commonly rectangular or round pocket into which a mating tenon is inserted. Mortises can be blind (stop inside the wood thickness), through, or open on one end.

PARTICLEBOARD A panel made of wood particles and glue.

PILOT HOLE A small, drilled hole used as a guide and pressure relief for screw insertion, or to locate additional drilling work like countersinking and counterboring.

PLYWOOD Panel made by laminating layers of wood.

QUARTERSAWN A stable lumber cut where the growth rings on the board's end run more vertically across the end than horizontal and the grain on the face looks straight; also called straight-grained or riftsawn.

RABBET A milled cut which leaves a flat step parallel to, but recessed from, the wood's surface.

RAIL The name of the horizontal parts of a door frame.

RIP To cut parallel to the grain of a board.

SAPWOOD The new wood in a tree, located between the core (heartwood) and bark. Usually lighter in color.

SCARF JOINT A joint that increases the overall length of wood by joining two pieces at their ends, commonly by gluing together two unusually long bevels in their faces or edges.

SCRIBE To make layout lines or index marks using a knife or awl.

SHOULDER The perpendicular face of a step cut like a rabbet which bears against a mating joint part to stabilize the joint.

SOFTWOOD Wood from coniferous evergreen trees, no matter what the density (yew is a softwood).

SPLINE A flat, thin strip of wood that fits into mating grooves between two parts to reinforce the joint between them.

STAIN A pigment or dye used to color wood through saturation, or, a discoloration in wood from fungus or chemicals.

STILE The name of the vertical parts of a door frame.

TENON The male part of a mortise and tenon joint, commonly rectangular or round, but not restricted to those shapes.

TONGUE AND GROOVE Joinery method in which one board is cut with a protruding groove and another is cut with a matching groove along its edge.

TWISTING A drying defect in lumber that causes it to twist so the faces at the end of the board are in a different plane.

VENEER A thin sheet of wood bonded to another material.

WIDTH JOINT A joint which makes a unit of the parts by joining them edge to edge to increase the overall width of wood.

Cream Can Lamp

This delightful little lamp is reminiscent of the milk or cream can farmers used to hold dairy products. The can is made of four pieces of laminated poplar and turned to its final dimensions. There is a hole through the middle to facilitate all the electrical connections. To assure a hole with a true center, the hole is "drilled" before the can is glued and laminated. Even though the cream can described here has a stained finish, it could have been painted and would look just as good.

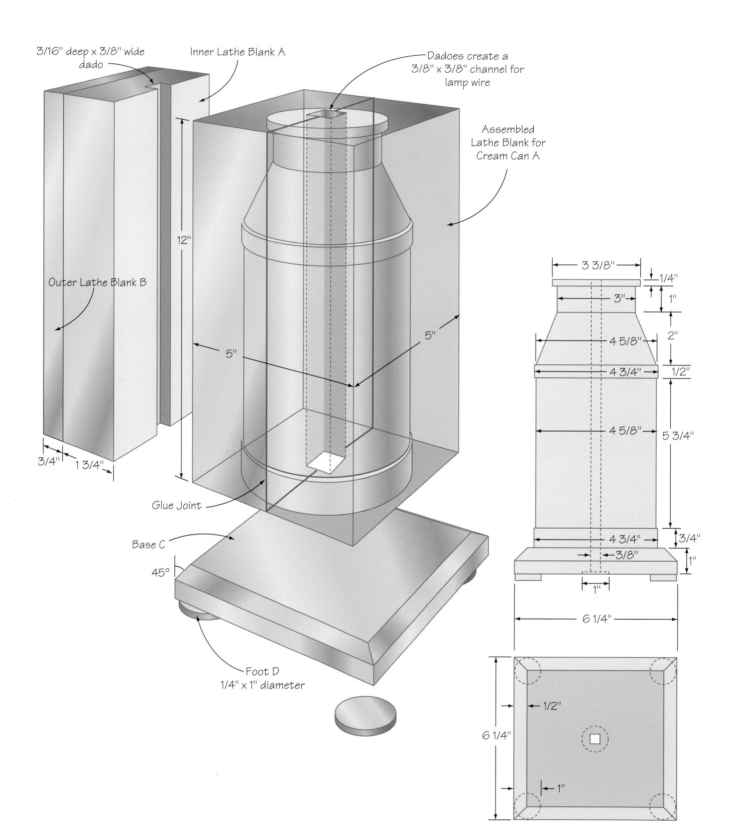

3/16" deep x 3/8" wide dado

Inner Lathe Blank A

Dadoes create a 3/8" x 3/8" channel for lamp wire

Assembled Lathe Blank for Cream Can A

12"

Outer Lathe Blank B

5"

5"

3/4" 1 3/4"

Glue Joint

Base C

45°

Foot D
1/4" x 1" diameter

3 3/8"

1/4"

1"

3"

4 5/8"

2"

4 3/4"

1/2"

4 5/8"

5 3/4"

4 3/4"

3/4"

3/8"

1"

1"

6 1/4"

1/2"

6 1/4"

1"

Cutting List • Cream Can Lamp

REF.	QTY.	PART	STOCK	THICK	WIDTH	LENGTH	COMMENTS
A	2	Can Parts	⁸⁄₄ Poplar	4¾	4¾	12	
B	2	Can Parts	⁴⁄₄ Poplar	4¾	4¾	12	
C	1	Base	⁵⁄₄ Cherry	¹¹⁄₁₆	6¼	6¼	
D	4	Feet	1" dia. dowel	¼	1" dia.		
	2	Lathe-Mounting Blanks	⅜" dia. dowel			1"	For mounting the blank on the lathe

Hardware

E	2	¼" Copper Tubing for Handles
	4	Decorative Screws to Attach Handles
	1 set	Lamp Hardware (socket, etc.)

Supplies

	Carpenter's Glue
	Maple Stain
	Gloss Ployurethane
	Satin Polyurethane
	#400 Wet/Dry Paper

REQUIRED TOOLS

Table saw

Lathe

Drill press

Clamps

Sander

Body Blank Assembly

The can blank is made from two 8/4 inner pieces of poplar and two 4/4 outer pieces glued and clamped together. On a table saw, cut each piece to a dimension of 4¾"×12". As indicated in the technical drawing, the two inner 8/4 members have ⅜"×³⁄₁₆" dadoes cut into them to allow for the passage of the threaded rod during electrical assembly. Glue and clamp the four pieces together, and after the glue has cured, cut two ⅜"×1" dowels and glue them into ⅜"×⅜" holes drilled at each end of the can blank. These dowels will serve as mounting plugs for the blank on the lathe.

Turning the Body

Find the center on each mounting plug, center punch the marks and mount the blank between centers of your lathe. Using a roughing gouge, turn the blank to a cylinder to a diameter of 4¾" as shown in the technical drawing.

Now is the time to mark all the turning dimensions on the blank. Turn the 4⅝" dimension on the cylinder. Square up each corner with a parting and beading gouge. Using a parting tool, determine the 3" and 3⅜" depths. Clean out these areas with a ⅜" gouge. Taper the top portion of the can, and round over the top ¼" with the parting and beading tool.

You'll notice there's some stock left over at the top of the can, (directly above the ¼" bead). Using a parting tool, cut down into the top of the can until there is about ¾" material remaining. Remove the can from the lathe, saw off the scrap piece and sand the top smooth.

Making the Base

Cut a piece of 5/4 stock to the dimensions in the cutting list. For this part, I used a piece of cherry, to add a little contrast. Set your saw to 45° and cut the four ½" chamfers. Determine the center of the base and with a Forstner bit, bore a 1"×¼" hole in the bottom. Then with a ⅜" bit, bore a hole completely through the base.

Make the four small feet from four chunks of 1" dowel, each ¼" thick, and glue them to the base. Once the glue is dry, sand everything smooth.

Lamp Assembly

This project is held together by the threaded rod used in wiring the lamp. Most likely you will have to saw a piece of rod to size. Before you do this, make sure you have all the mechanical parts on hand so you can get an accurate measurement as to the length of the rod.

Forming the Handles

Make the two handles out of ¼" copper tubing. Copper is a very malleable and easy material to use and can be easily shaped to the outer surface of the can. Wait until you've stained, but not finished, the cream can to attach the handles to the lamp. That way, you'll protect the copper against surface oxidation.

Finishing

I used a maple wiping stain for the can itself but left the cherry base a contrasting "natural." After the stain dries, give both pieces a coat of gloss ployurethane, followed by two coats of satin polyurethane. Between each coat, lightly sand with 400-girt wet/dry paper.

Candlesticks

These little beauties will light up a table for a romantic dinner for two, or they can be used just for decorations. The turning designs or dimensions are not sacred and can be changed to fit the desires of the turner.

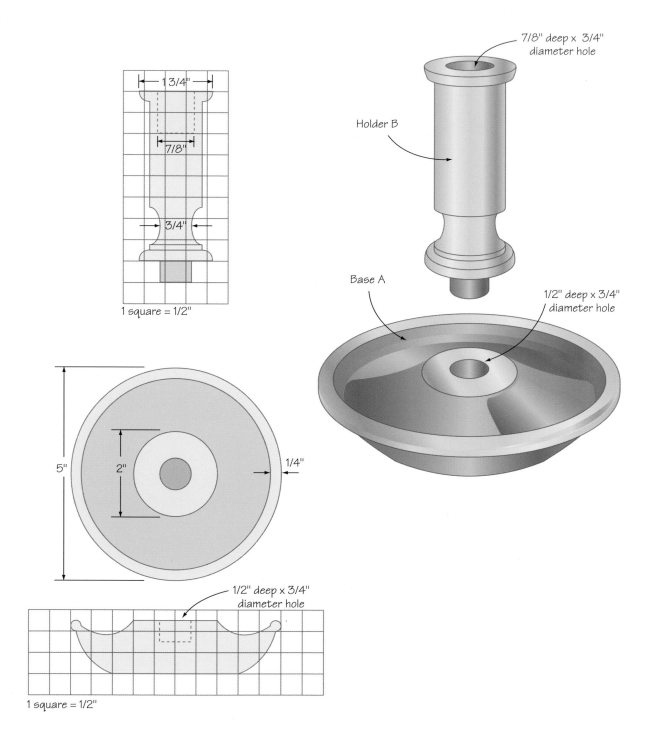

1 3/4"

7/8"

3/4"

1 square = 1/2"

7/8" deep x 3/4"
diameter hole

Holder B

Base A

1/2" deep x 3/4"
diameter hole

5"

2"

1/4"

1/2" deep x 3/4"
diameter hole

1 square = 1/2"

Cutting List • Candlesticks

REF.	QTY.	PART	STOCK	THICK	WIDTH	LENGTH	COMMENTS
	1	Base	Walnut	¼	5¼	5¼	
	1	Holder	Cherry	¾	1¾	4½	

Hardware

	2	Brass Candle Eyelets (Constantine's #99U8)					

Supplies

		Carpenter's Glue					
		Gloss Polyurethane					
		Satin Polyurethane					
		#600 Wet/Dry Paper					

Building the Base

Cut the base to an overall rough dimension of 5¼" square. Scribe a 5" circle on the blank, and cut it out on a band saw. Mount the blank on your lathe using a faceplate, either by screwing the base to the faceplate, or by using double-sided tape (see photo 1). The beauty of the double-sided tape is that there are no screw holes to deal with after the lathe work is completed. Using a bowl gouge, true up the outer edge of the base to a dimension of 5" (see photo 2). Mark the ¼" dimension on the side. Using a parting tool, make a cut about ⅛" deep, ¼" down from the top edge.

With the gouge, shape the outer edge similar to the shape shown in the technical drawing. Then, again with the gouge, shape the top surface (see photo 3). If you have a Jacob's chuck that can be attached to the tail stock of your lathe, now is the time to bore a ¾" hole, to a depth of ½" (see photo 4). If not, sand the base, take it off the faceplate and bore the hole on the drill press. Either way you do it, use a ¾" Forstner bit for a clean, accurate hole.

REQUIRED TOOLS

Band saw

Lathe

Jacob's chuck

Drill press

1 Mount the candlestick base to the lathe faceplate with double-sided tape.

Making the Holder

Mount the 1¾"-square cherry blank between centers of your lathe. Using a roughing gouge, turn the blank to an overall diameter of 1¾". Mark the ¼" dimension from the top followed by a dimension of 3½", and then ¼" and ½" respectively. If these measurements are done correctly, an overall size of 4½" inches results.

Using a plain parting tool, and starting ¼" from the top, make a cut to a depth of 1¼" inches. Do the same thing 3½" inches down the holder toward the bottom. With a gouge or a skew chisel turn the space between parting cuts to a 1¼" diameter.

Mark a ½" dimension for the mounting stub as shown at the bottom of the holder. Then with a parting tool, make a ¾" cut. Clean out the remainder of the stub with a ⅜" gouge. Note that this ¾" dimension has to mate with the hole bored in the base. Since it's desirable to have a good fit, make a fit check by temporarily removing the blank from the lathe and fitting it into the base. If the fit is satisfactory, reinstall the blank on the lathe, mark the ⅞" dimension and shape the bottom section of the holder with a ⅜" gouge.

All that now remains to be done is to roll over both top and bottom ¼" edges with a ⅜" parting and beading gouge (see photo 5). Sand the holder and remove it from the lathe. Bore a ⅞"-diameter hole in the top with a Forstner bit to accommodate the brass candle eyelet ,which is the last thing to be installed after all finishing operations are completed. Finally, glue the holder to the base.

2 True up the candle base edge with a deep gouge chisel.

3 Here you see the candle base in the process of being gouged out.

Finishing

There are many finishes that can be applied to a project such as this. For example you might like a plain wax finish, a rubbed bee's wax finish or an oil finish; however, for this project, I used one coat of gloss polyurethane, followed by two coats of satin polyurethane. Between coats I sanded lightly with 600-grit wet/dry paper.

Installing the Brass Eyelet

The brass eyelet should be pressed into the candle hole using uniform pressure. An uneven pressure can result in splitting the holder. The eyelet can be easily inserted using the drill press as an arbor press to apply uniform pressure.

4 While still mounted on the lathe, bore the center hole in the candle base with a ¾" Forstner bit.

5 Here's the completed candle holder spindle still mounted on the lathe.

Candle Stand

This attractive stand features a central turned post and a round top. As you can see, not only will this stand display candles to great effect, but it can be used as a plant pedestal or to hold other items. Although I built this particular piece from red oak, other hardwoods, such as cherry, can be used.

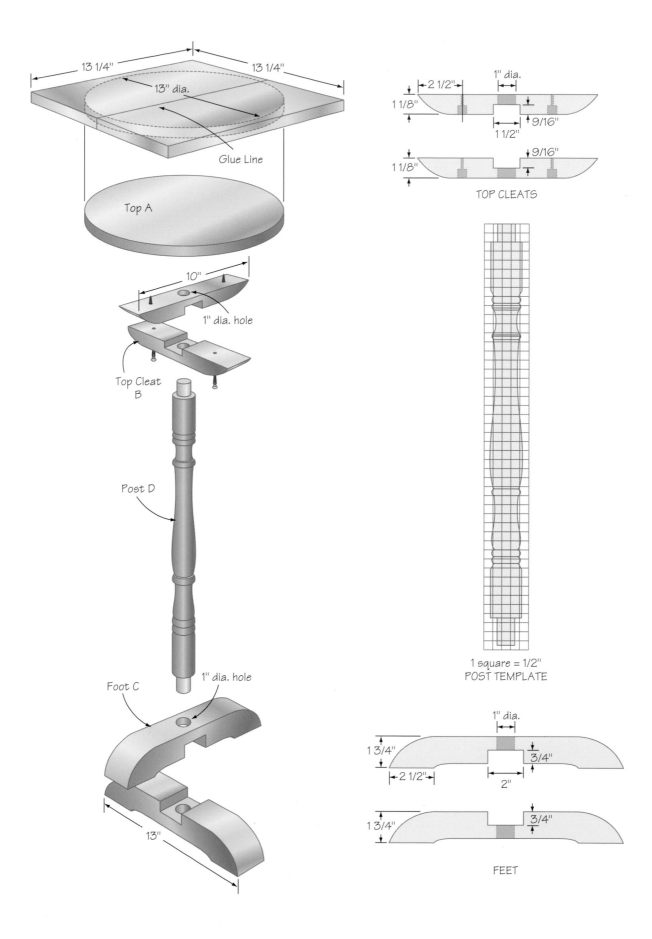

13 1/4"

13 1/4"

13" dia.

Glue Line

Top A

10"

1" dia. hole

Top Cleat
B

Post D

Foot C

1" dia. hole

13"

2 1/2"

1" dia.

1 1/8"

9/16"

1 1/2"

1 1/8"

9/16"

TOP CLEATS

1 square = 1/2"
POST TEMPLATE

1" dia.

1 3/4"

3/4"

2 1/2"

2"

1 3/4"

3/4"

FEET

Cutting List • Candle Stand

REF.	QTY.	PART	STOCK	THICK	WIDTH	LENGTH	COMMENTS
A	1	Top	4/4 Red Oak	3/4	13 1/4	13 1/4	Final dimension is 13" in diameter
B	2	Top Cleats	Red Oak	1 1/8	1 1/2	10	
C	2	Feet	Red Oak	1 3/4	2	13	
D	1	Post	Red Oak	1 3/4	1 3/4	24 1/4	Length includes tenons on ends

Hardware

	1	#8 RH Screw for Mounting Circle Routing Jig
	4	#8 x 1 1/4 Round Head Screws

Supplies

	Carpenter's Glue
	Golden Oak Stain
	Gloss Polyurethane
	Satin Polyurethane
	#400 Wet/Dry Paper
	Furniture Wax
	0000 Steel Wool

Making the Top

Glue up and clamp sufficient 4/4 stock to make a 13¼"-square blank. Flip the top, good side down, and determine the center point of the blank. Using a compass, draw a 13" circle. With a saber saw or band saw, cut around the circumference of the circle (make sure you stay at least ⅛" to the outside). You now have a rough-sawn edge that has to be smoothed. This operation can be done using a router and the simple circle-routing jig as described in Tools and Techniques.

Routing the Top

Set the depth of the straight router bit ¼" or less for the first pass. Attach the router jig arm to the candle stand top center point with a #8 RH screw. Take care that the screw allows the arm to rotate 360° (also make sure that the pivot screw does not penetrate completely through the top). Rout in a counterclockwise direction until the entire circumference is traversed. Lower the bit another ¼" and again rout the circumference. Continue this operation until the entire edge is routed smooth.

Round over the top and bottom edges of the top to soften its looks and to eliminate sharp edges. Use a ½" roundover bit for the top edge and a ¼" roundover bit for the bottom edge.

Required Tools

- Saber saw or band saw
- Router
- Circle routing jig
- Drill or drill press
- Lathe
- Sander (or sandpaper and block)

Making the Cleats

Two cleats are needed to support the top and to connect to the center post. These are positioned 90° to each other. Cut a cross lap on each of these cleats. Ensure that both pieces fit together snugly at a 90° angle (see photo 1). Shape a curve on the four ends and sand smooth. Temporarily assemble the cleats and determine the center point where they are joined. With a 1" Forstner bit, bore a hole through the center point of the two cleats.

Making the Feet

Each foot is made from 1¾"×2"×13" stock. Cut a cross lap in both pieces. Also cut a ¼"×8" clearance on each bottom. Shape all four ends as shown in the technical drawing. As was done above with the cleats, temporarily assemble the feet, determine the center and bore a 1" hole through the centers of both feet (see photo 2).

Turning the Post

Mount the post blank between the lathe centers. Turn two stubs on either end. Mark off the 1¾"×1¾"×3" dimension on each end. Using a skew chisel, turn a pommel off each square. With a roughing gouge, size the stock between pommels to a dimension of 1⅝". Turn the remainder of the design as shown in the technical drawing, and sand smooth (see photo 3).

Assembly

Glue and clamp both the foot and top cleat assemblies, and glue these to the post. The 1½" end of the center post is inserted into the foot assembly. Make sure that the straight edges of the cleats and feet line up in the same directions. Finally, assemble the top cleat assembly to the candle stand top using four #8×1¼" round head screws.

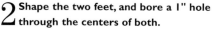
1 Here you see the two cleats and the two feet. Make sure that the lap joints fit snugly together.

2 Shape the two feet, and bore a 1" hole through the centers of both.

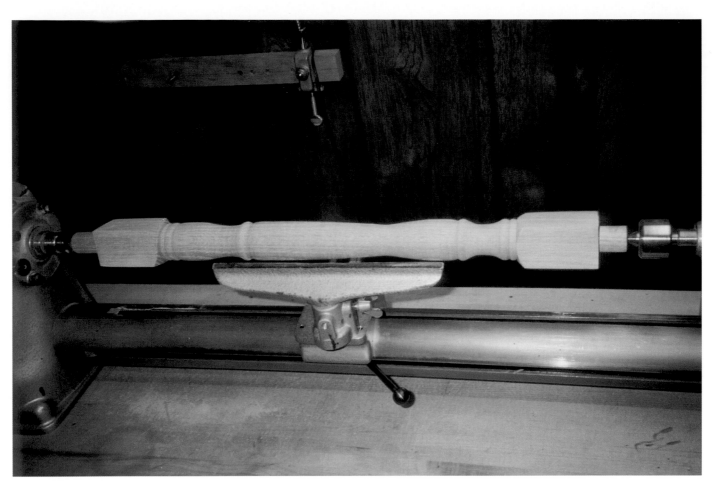

3 Here you see the turned post still mounted on the lathe, just prior to final sanding.

Finishing

To finish the stand, apply one coat of golden oak stain followed by a coat of gloss polyurethane and two coats of satin polyurethane. Between coats, lightly sand with 400-grit wet/dry paper and wipe the project with a tack rag. Once the final coat is thoroughly dry, rub the stand to a final finish using wax and 0000 fine steel wool.

Pedestal Table

One of my sons had just purchased a house and he asked me to build him a table for a dining area adjacent to the kitchen. Since the area was relatively compact, the table had to fit the dimensions of the area. We settled on a 36" round pedestal table. The table is made from 5/4 red oak; however, any of a number of hard- or softwoods can be used (cherry, maple or pine), depending upon your taste and requirements.

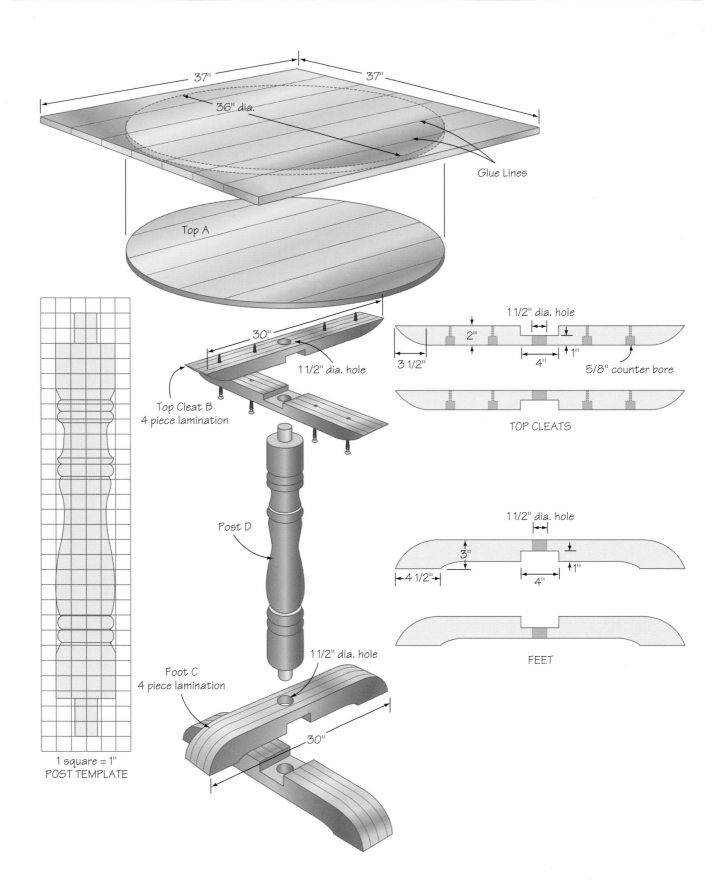

37"

37"

36" dia.

Glue Lines

Top A

30"

1 1/2" dia. hole

Top Cleat B
4 piece lamination

1 1/2" dia. hole

2"

3 1/2"

4"

1"

5/8" counter bore

TOP CLEATS

Post D

1 1/2" dia. hole

3"

4 1/2"

4"

1"

FEET

Foot C
4 piece lamination

1 1/2" dia. hole

30"

1 square = 1"
POST TEMPLATE

Cutting List • Pedestal Table

REF.	QTY.	PART	STOCK	THICK	WIDTH	LENGTH	COMMENTS
A	1	Top	5/4 Red Oak	1 1/16	37	37	Glued-up dimensions
B	2	Cleats	5/4 Red Oak	2	4	30	Glued-up dimensions
C	2	Feet	5/4 Red Oak	3	4	30	Glued-up dimensions
D	1	Post	5/4 Red Oak	4	4	28	Glued-up dimensions

Hardware

	4	#8 x 2" Flathead Screws
	4	#8 x 1½" Falthead Screws
	8	#8 x 2" Round Head Screws

Supplies

		Carpenter's Glue
		Golden Oak Stain
		Gloss Ployurethane
		Satin Polyurethane
		#400 Wet/Dry Paper
		Cabinet Wax
		0000 Steel Wool

Required Tools

- Jointer
- Clamps
- Compass
- Saber saw or band saw
- Router
- Circle routing jig
- Sander (or sandpaper and block)
- Drill or drill press
- Lathe

Making the Top

Edge-glue and clamp six or seven pieces of 5/4 jointed stock to make a 37"-square blank. After the glue has dried, flip the top good side down and determine the center point of the blank on the bottom side. Using a beam compass, draw a 36" circle (set the beam compass to 18").

With a saber saw or band saw, cut around the circumference of the circle (make sure you stay at least ⅛" to the outside of the scribed line). You now have a rough-sawn edge that has to be smoothed. This operation can be done using a router and the simple circle-routing jig as shown in Tools and Techniques.

Routing the Top

With a straight ⅜" router bit in the router, set the router's depth to ¼" or less for the first pass. Attach the router jig arm to the tabletop center point with a #8 round head screw. Take care that the screw allows the arm to rotate 360° (also make sure that the pivot screw does not penetrate completely through the tabletop). Rout in a counterclockwise direction until the entire circumference is traversed. Lower the bit another ¼" and again rout the circumference. Continue lowering the bit until the entire edge is routed smooth.

Round over the top edge of the tabletop with a ½" roundover bit, and the bottom edge with a ¼" roundover bit.

Making the Cleats

In order to support the tabletop and to connect the top to the pedestal, two cleats are necessary, positioned 90° to each other. These are made by laminating four pieces, each 2"×31", of 5/4 wood. Trim both cleats to 30". Cut a cross lap on each of these cleats, one on the top and one on the bottom. Make sure that both pieces fit together snugly at a 90° angle. Round over all four ends of the cleats and sand smooth. Temporarily assemble the cleats and determine the center point where they are joined. Using a 1½" Forstner bit, bore a hole through the center point of the two cleats.

Making the Feet

Each foot is made from four 3"×30" pieces of 5/4 stock laminated together. Cut a cross lap in both pieces and also cut a ½"×20" recess on each bottom. As with the cleats, temporarily assemble the feet, determine the center and bore an 1½" hole through the centers.

Turning the Post

Laminate four 4"×28" pieces of 5/4 stock. Mount the blank between the centers of the lathe and, with a roughing gouge, turn a 4" cylinder. Turn two stubs on either end, 2"×1½" for the top and 2½"×1½" for the bottom. Turn the remainder of the design as shown in the technical drawing, or turn your own design—there's nothing sacred about my design!

Assembly

Counterbore four ⅝"-diameter holes in each cleat to a depth of ⅝". Drill an oversized hole (somewhat larger than the shank dimension of a #8 wood screw) in each of the counterbores to accommodate a #8×2" round head screw. The oversized holes are necessary to allow for seasonal shrinking and swelling of wood, and thus avoid any cracks in the tabletop.

Place the first cleat on the top of the pedestal, and drill and screw the cleat to the pedestal (use two #8×2" flathead screws). With two #8×1½" flathead screws, screw the second cleat to the other cleat. Assemble the feet to the pedestal in the same manner as the cleats were assembled, taking care that the feet go in the same direction as the cleats.

Finally, assemble the pedestal assembly to the bottom of the tabletop using eight, #8×2" round head screws.

Finishing

To achieve the same finish that I used, apply two coats of golden oak stain, followed by a coat of gloss polyurethane and two coats of satin polyurethane. Between coats, lightly sand the project with 400-grit wet/dry paper, wiping the table after each sanding with a tack rag. When the finish is thoroughly dry, rub down the entire project using a good cabinet wax and 0000 superfine steel wool. Finally, buff to final finish with a soft cloth.

Metric Conversions

U.S. UNITS TO METRIC EQUIVALENTS			METRIC UNITS TO U.S. EQUIVALENTS		
To convert from	Multiply by	To get	To convert from	Multiply by	To get
Inches	25.4	Millimeters	Millimeters	0.0394	Inches
Inches	2.54	Centimeters	Centimeters	0.3937	Inches
Feet	30.48	Centimeters	Centimeters	0.0328	Feet
Feet	0.3048	Meters	Meters	3.2808	Feet
Yards	0.9144	Meters	Meters	1.0936	Yards
Square inches	6.4516	Square centimeters	Square centimeters	0.1550	Square inches
Square feet	0.0929	Square meters	Square meters	10.764	Square feet Square
yards	0.8361	Square meters	Square meters	1.1960	Square yards
Acres	0.4047	Hectares	Hectares	2.4711	Acres
Cubic inches	16.387	Cubic centimeters	Cubic centimeters	0.0610	Cubic inches
Cubic feet	0.0283	Cubic meters	Cubic meters	35.315	Cubic feet
Cubic feet	28.316	Liters	Liters	0.0353	Cubic feet
Cubic yards	0.7646	Cubic meters	Cubic meters	1.308	Cubic yards
Cubic yards	764.55	Liters	Liters	0.0013	Cubic yards
Ounces (fluid)	0.0296	Liters	Liters	33.784	Ounces (fluid)
Pints	0.4732	Liters	Liters	2.1133	Pints
Quarts	0.9464	Liters	Liters	1.0566	Quarts
Gallons	3.7854	Liters	Liters	0.2642	Gallons
Ounces (weight)	28.350	Grams	Grams	0.3527	Ounces (weight)
Pounds	0.4536	Kilograms	Kilograms	2.2046	Pounds

Lumber

WOOD SIZE (MILLIMETERS)	NEAREST U.S. EQUIVALENT (INCHES)
25 x 75	1 x 3
50 x 100	2 x 4
50 x 150	2 x 6
50 x 200	2 x 8
50 x 250	2 x 10
50 x 300	2 x 12

Fractions to Metric Equivalents

INCHES	MILLIMETERS	INCHES	MILLIMETERS	INCHES	MILLIMETERS	INCHES	MILLIMETERS
1/64	0.396875	17/64	6.746875	33/64	13.096880	49/64	19.446880
1/32	0.793750	9/32	7.143750	17/32	13.493750	25/32	19.843750
3/64	1.190625	19/64	7.540625	35/64	13.890630	51/64	20.240630
1/16	1.587500	5/16	7.937500	9/16	14.287500	13/16	20.637500
5/64	1.984375	21/64	8.334375	37/64	14.684380	53/64	21.034380
3/32	2.381250	11/32	8.731250	19/32	15.081250	27/32	21.431250
7/64	2.778125	23/64	9.128125	39/64	15.478130	55/64	21.828130
1/8	3.175000	3/8	9.525000	5/8	15.875000	7/8	22.225000
9/64	3.571875	25/64	9.921875	41/64	16.271880	57/64	22.621880
5/32	3.968750	13/32	10.318750	21/32	16.668750	29/32	23.018750
11/64	4.365625	27/64	10.715630	43/64	17.065630	59/64	23.415630
3/16	4.762500	7/16	11.112500	11/16	17.462500	15/16	23.812500
13/64	5.159375	29/64	11.509380	45/64	17.859380	61/64	24.209380
7/32	5.556250	15/32	11.906250	23/32	18.256250	31/32	24.606250
15/64	5.953125	31/64	12.303130	47/64	18.653130	63/64	25.003130
1/4	6.350000	1/2	12.700000	3/4	19.050000	1	25.400000

Nested Tables

These attractive tables can sit beside a chair or sofa and be used as side tables, or when guests arrive, they can be used as serving trays. Made of solid cherry, they feature turned tapered legs and a polyurethane finish. The legs require the use of a lathe. If one is not available, they can be tapered on the table saw and will still be very attractive.

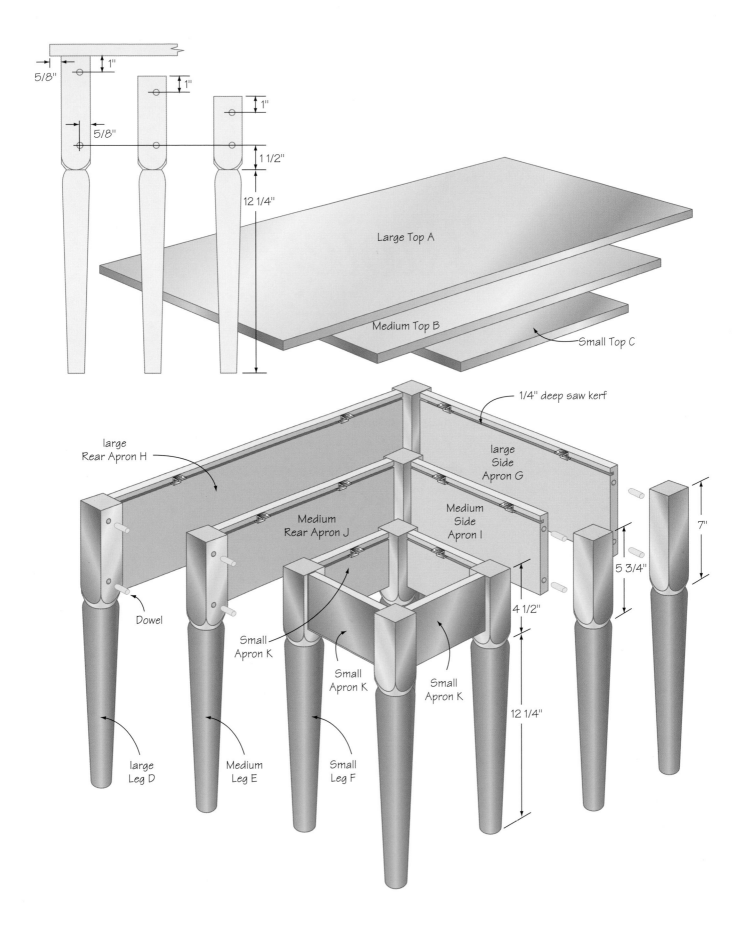

5/8"

1"

1"

1"

5/8"

1 1/2"

12 1/4"

Large Top A

Medium Top B

Small Top C

1/4" deep saw kerf

large
Rear Apron H

large
Side
Apron G

Medium
Rear Apron J

Medium
Side
Apron I

Small
Apron K

Small
Apron K

Small
Apron K

7"

5 3/4"

4 1/2"

12 1/4"

Dowel

large
Leg D

Medium
Leg E

Small
Leg F

Cutting List • Nested Tables

REF.	QTY.	PART	STOCK	THICK	WIDTH	LENGTH	COMMENTS
Tops							
A	1	Large Top	Cherry	¾	15	23	
B	1	Medium Top	Cherry	¾	13	17	
C	1	Small Top	Cherry	¾	11	10¾	
Legs							
D	4	Large Legs	Cherry	1¾	1¾	19¼	
E	4	Medium Legs	Cherry	1¾	1¾	18	
F	4	Small Legs	Cherry	1¾	1¾	16¾	
Aprons							
G	2	Large Side Aprons	Cherry	¾	6	10	
H	1	Large Rear Apron	Cherry	¾	6	18	
I	2	Medium Side Aprons	Cherry	¾	4¾	8	
J	1	Medium Rear Apron	Cherry	¾	4¾	11	
K	4	Small Aprons	Cherry	¾	3½	6	

Hardware

	40	1½" x ⅜" Diameter Dowels	
	26	Fasteners (Woodcraft #27N10)	

Supplies

Carpenter's Glue

Gloss Polyurethane

Satin Polyurethane

#400 Wet/Dry Paper

Cabinet Wax

0000 Steel Wool

REQUIRED TOOLS

Table or circular saw

Jointer

Clamps

Router

Sander (or sandpaper and block)

Lathe

Doweling Jig

Drill or drill press

Making the Tops

Cut, joint, glue and clamp stock to make up the three different top blanks. After the glue has dried, trim each of the blanks to their respective finished dimensions as listed in the bill of materials. Sand each blank. With a ½" router roundover bit, round over the top edges of each. Reverse each blank and round over the bottom edges using a ¼" roundover bit. Finish sand each top.

Making the Aprons

There are ten different aprons required for the three tables in this project. Cut each of them to the dimensions listed in the bill of materials. With a table saw, cut a ¼" kerf on the rear of each apron as shown in the technical drawing. Finally, sand each apron.

Making the Legs

Cut the three sets of leg blanks to size as listed in the bill of materials. Find the center point on the ends of each blank. Mount the blank on the lathe. Lay out the 12¼" dimension, and with a roughing gouge, turn this section to a 1⅝" diameter. As you can see in the technical drawing, each set has this 12¼" dimension.

Using a skew chisel, turn a pummel on the bottom portion of the square section. With a skew chisel, score the section immediately below the pummel to a depth of about ⅛". Turn a modified bead on the top portion of the turned section. Using a gouge, taper the leg to a 1" diameter. Designate the location of each leg, then lay out and bore the holes.

Leg and Apron Assembly

The holes previously bored in the legs have to be transferred accurately to the aprons. To accomplish this effectively, use the doweling jig as described in Tools and Techniques. Position the leg and apron as shown in the instructions for the doweling jig, insert the ⅜" diameter dowel centers into the holes bored in the leg, and press the apron into the leg. Bore out the holes now marked on the edge of the apron. Place two 1½" diameter dowels into the two holes and check for a good fit between leg and apron. If all went well, a perfect fit results. Continue this process until all apron holes are bored. Glue and clamp the dowels to the legs and side aprons.

After the glue has dried, glue and clamp the rear and front aprons to the legs. As can be seen, the small table is the only one that has a front apron.

Final Assembly

All that remains to complete construction of this project is to attach the tops to the leg-apron assembly. Invert each of the tops on a bench and center each of the respective leg-apron assemblies on the top. Insert the tabletop fasteners into the saw-kerfs, mark and drill the pilot holes for the fasteners and screw them in. It is only necessary to use two fasteners on each side of the small table. The other two tables will require ten fasteners each.

Finishing

To finish this project, apply one coat of gloss polyurethane, followed by two coats of satin polyurethane. Lightly sand the tables between coats with 400-grit wet/dry paper. After each sanding wipe the tables with a tack rag. After the finish has dried, apply a coat of cabinet wax with 0000 steel wool and buff to a final sheen with a soft cloth.

Common Stains and Topcoats

STAINS

STAIN TYPE	FORM	PREPARATION	CHARACTERISTICS
Pigment stains			
Oil-based	Liquid	Mix thoroughly	Apply with rag, brush or spray; resists fading.
Water-based	Liquid	Mix thoroughly	Apply with rag, brush or spray; resists fading; water cleanup.
Gel	Gel	Ready to use	Apply with rag; won't raise grain; easy to use; no drips or runs.
Water-based gel	Gel	Ready to use	Apply with rag; easy to use; no drips or runs.
Japan color	Concentrated liquid	Mix thoroughly	Used for tinting stains, paints, varnish, lacquer.
Dye stains			
Water-based	Powder	Mix with water	Apply with rag, brush or spray; deep penetrating; best resistance of dye stains; good clarity; raises grain.
Oil-based	Powder	Mix with toluol, lacquer thinner, turpentine or naphtha	Apply with rag, brush or spray; penetrating; does not raise grain; dries slowly.
Alcohol-based	Powder	Mix with alcohol	Apply with rag, brush or spray; penetrating; does not raise grain; dries quickly; lap marks sometimes a problem.
NGR	Liquid	Mix thoroughly	Apply with rag, brush or spray (use retarder if wiping or brushing); good clarity; does not raise grain.

TOPCOATS

FINISH TYPE	FORM	PREPARATION	CHARACTERISTICS	DRY TIME
Shellac	Liquid	Mix thoroughly	Dries quickly; economical; available either clear or amber-colored; high gloss luster; affected by water, alcohol and heat.	2 hours
Shellac flakes	Dry flakes	Mix with alcohol	Dries quickly; economical (mix only what is needed); color choices from amber to clear; high gloss luster; affected by water, alcohol and heat.	2 hours
Lacquer	Liquid	Mix with thinner for spraying	Dries quickly; clear (shaded lacquers available); high gloss luster, but flattening agents available; durable; moisture resistant.	30 minutes
Varnish	Liquid	Mix thoroughly	Dries slowly; amber color; gloss, semi-gloss and satin lusters; very good durability and moisture resistance; flexible.	3 to 6 hours
Polyurethane	Liquid	Mix thoroughly	Dries slowly; clear to amber colors; gloss, semi-gloss and satin lusters; excellent durability and moisture resistance; flexible.	3 to 6 hours
Water-based polyurethane	Liquid	Mix thoroughly	Dries quickly; clear; won't yellow; gloss and satin lusters; moisture and alcohol resistant; low odor.	2 hours
Oil/Varnish	Liquid	Ready to use	Dries slowly; amber color; satin luster; poor moisture resistance; easy to use.	20 to 24 hours
Wiping varnish	Liquid	Mix thoroughly	Dries slowly; amber color; satin luster; poor moisture resistance; easy to use.	8 to 10 hours

NOTE: Dry times are based on a temperature of 70° Fahrenheit and 40 percent relative humidity. Lower temperature and/or higher relative humidity can increase drying time.

Spiral Staircase Table

Some years ago, my wife and I spent a week cross-country skiing in Stowe, Vermont. While there, we stayed at the Trapp Family Farm (as in The Sound Of Music*). In the library of the main lodge, we discovered what I call a spiral staircase table. I had never seen another like it. Subsequently, I learned the original use of such a piece was as a step stool to reach books located high out of reach in a formal library; however, this one was used as a table to hold a lamp and various small items of interest. Over the years, the memory of this table remained with me. Recently, I decided to design and build one. The only caution I can give about this piece is, if you decide to build it, don't use it as a step stool! This attractive table is made from cherry wood and has a natural finish to showcase the beauty of the wood. For those who like to do wood turning, this project features lots of spindle turning on the lathe.*

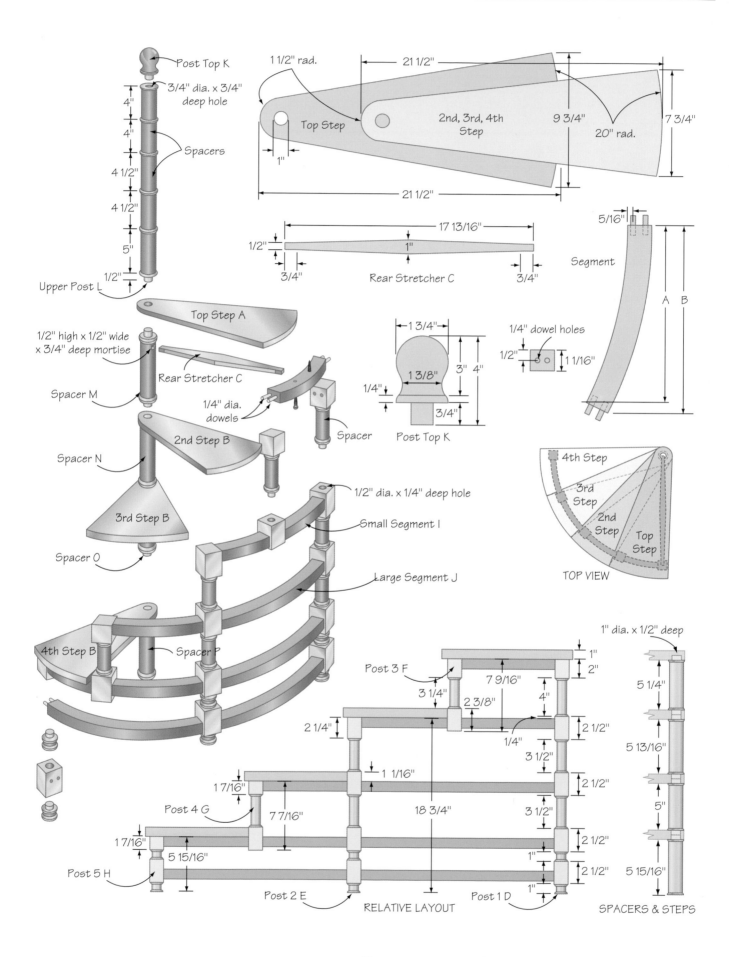

Post Top K

3/4" dia. x 3/4" deep hole

4"

4"

4 1/2"

Spacers

4 1/2"

5"

1/2"

Upper Post L

1 1/2" rad.

21 1/2"

Top Step

2nd, 3rd, 4th Step

9 3/4"

7 3/4"

20" rad.

1"

21 1/2"

17 13/16"

1/2"

1"

3/4"

Rear Stretcher C

3/4"

5/16"

Segment

A   B

Top Step A

1/2" high x 1/2" wide x 3/4" deep mortise

Spacer M

Rear Stretcher C

1/4" dia. dowels

1 3/4"

3"   4"

1/4" dowel holes

1/2"

1 1/16"

Spacer

1/4"

1 3/8"

3/4"

Post Top K

2nd Step B

Spacer N

3rd Step B

Spacer O

1/2" dia. x 1/4" deep hole

Small Segment I

Large Segment J

4th Step

3rd Step

2nd Step

Top Step

TOP VIEW

4th Step B

Spacer P

1" dia. x 1/2" deep

Post 3 F

1"

2"

7 9/16"

3 1/4"

2 3/8"

4"

2 1/4"

1/4"

2 1/2"

3 1/2"

1 1/16"

2 1/2"

1 7/16"

Post 4 G

7 7/16"

18 3/4"

3 1/2"

2 1/2"

1 7/16"

5 15/16"

1"

2 1/2"

1"

Post 5 H

Post 2 E

RELATIVE LAYOUT

Post 1 D

5 1/4"

5 13/16"

5"

5 15/16"

SPACERS & STEPS

Cutting List • Spiral Staircase Table

REF.	QTY.	PART	STOCK	THICK	WIDTH	LENGTH	COMMENTS
A	1	Top Step	Cherry	1 1/16	9 3/4	22	
B	3	2nd, 3rd & 4th Steps	Cherry	1 1/16	7 3/4	22	
C	1	Rear Stretcher	Cherry	1	1	17 13/16	Add an additional 1/2" for lathe work
D	1	Post #1	Cherry	1 1/2	1 1/2	25	
E	1	Post #2	Cherry	1 1/2	1 1/2	18 3/4	
F	1	Post #3	Cherry	1 1/2	1 1/2	7 9/16	
G	1	Post #4	Cherry	1 1/2	1 1/2	7 7/16	
H	1	Post #5	Cherry	1 1/2	1 1/2	5 15/16	
I	6	Small Segments	Cherry	1 1/16	1 1/2	6 1/4	Blank dimensions
J	4	Large Segments	Cherry	1 1/16	2 3/4	13 1/2	Blank dimensions
K	1	Post Top	Cherry	1 3/4	1 3/4	4	Add an additional 1/2" for lathe work
L	1	Upper Post	Cherry	1 3/4	1 3/4	22 1/2	
M	1	Spacer, Top & 2nd Step	Cherry	1 3/4	1 3/4	6 3/16	
N	1	Spacer, 2nd & 3rd Step	Cherry	1 3/4	1 3/4	6 3/4	
O	1	Spacer, 3rd & 4th Step	Cherry	1 3/4	1 3/4	5 15/16	
P	1	Spacer 4th Step & Floor	Cherry	1 3/4	1 3/4	6 7/16	

Hardware

	40	1/4" x 1" Dowels
	8	#8 x 1 3/4" Wood Screws

Supplies

- Carpenter's Glue
- Gloss Polyurethane
- Satin Polyurethane
- #400 Wet/Dry Paper
- Cabinet Wax
- 0000 Steel Wool

Required Tools

- Lathe
- Spindle sizing jig
- Drill
- Band saw or saber saw
- Dowel centers
- Sander (or sandpaper and block)

Lathe Work

There are 12 different spindles that have to be turned on a lathe. With the exception of the post top, most of the turning work is between center spindles. To quickly check the sizes of the spindles as you work, see the simple spindle-sizing jig as described in Tools and Techniques.

Before turning the spacer between the fourth step and the floor, bore a centered ½"-diameter hole, ¾" deep, 2¾" up from the floor. This hole will be used during final assembly of the rear stretcher.

Turning the Spacers

With a roughing gouge, and referring to the dimension chart below, turn all the spacers to an overall 1¾" diameter. With the exception of the spacer between the fourth step and floor, where there is only a stub on one end, turn 1"× ½" stubs on both ends of each spacer. These 1" diameter stubs should be turned using the actual measurement taken from the 1" Forstner bit that will be used later in the project. The reason for this is to obtain a snug fit between the spacers and the steps. Mark the C and D dimensions on the spacers and turn the G dimension (1½"). With a ⅜" beading and parting tool, round over the edges of C and D. Sand each spindle.

Turning the Upper Post

Mount the upper post blank on the lathe, and as was done with the spacers, turn the upper post blank to an overall 1¾" diameter (see photo 1). Mark all the dimensions on the blank and turn the 1"-diameter, ½"-long stub, again taking the 1" measurement from the Forstner bit selected for this project. Using a skew chisel, score a mark in the center of the four interior beads. Turn the 1½" diameters as indicated in the technical drawing (there are five such areas). Round over the beads with a parting and beading tool. Sand the post, and bore a ¾"× ¾" hole on the top end with a Forstner bit (see photo 2).

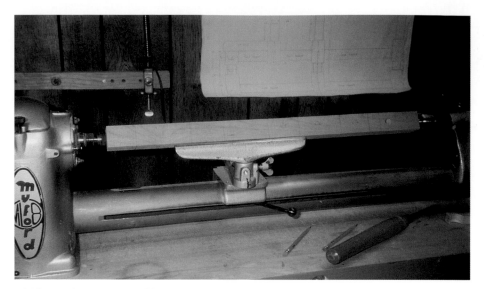

1 Mount the upper post blank on your lathe with all the dimensions marked.

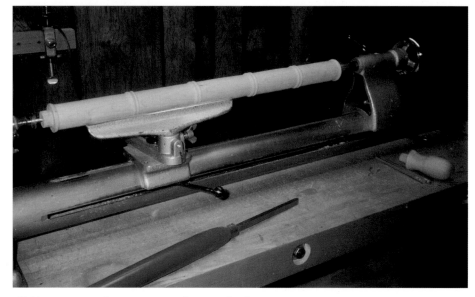

2 Here you see the upper post after turning is completed.

Spacers

SPACERS FROM	TOP & 2ND STEP	2ND & 3RD STEP	3RD & 4TH STEP	4TH STEP & FLOOR
A	1	1	1	1
B	½	½	½	½
C	¼	¼	¼	¼
D	¼	¼	¼	¼
E	½	½	½	N/A
F	1	1	1	N/A
G	1½	1½	1½	1½
H	1¾	1¾	1¾	1¾
I	5³⁄₁₆	5¾	4⁵⁄₁₆	5¹⁵⁄₁₆
J	6³⁄₁₆	6¾	5¹⁵⁄₁₆	6⁷⁄₁₆

Dimensions in inches

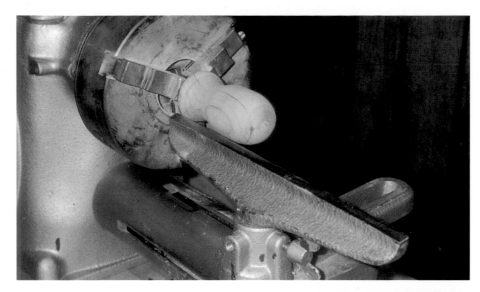

3 Transfer the stock for the post top to a three-jawed chuck and turn the ball end. Finally, sand it smooth.

Turning the Post Top

The post top can be turned using be-tween-the-centers turning or a combi-nation of between the centers and a chuck. I chose the latter method. Hold-ing the stock between-the-centers, turn the blank to a 1¾" cylinder. Lay out and mark all the dimensions as shown in the technical drawing. Cut the 1⅜" cove and round over the half bead. Transfer the stock to a three-jawed chuck and finish turning the ball end. Finally, sand the post top and glue it to the upper post (see photo 3).

Turning the Lower Posts

There are five different lower posts that require some turning. Each of these starts out as a 1½" square blank of the various lengths specified in the materials list. Mount each of these on the lathe and turn the 1" diameters as indicated in the technical drawing (see photos 4 and 5)

4 Here you see the longest of the lower posts while it is still mounted on the lathe.

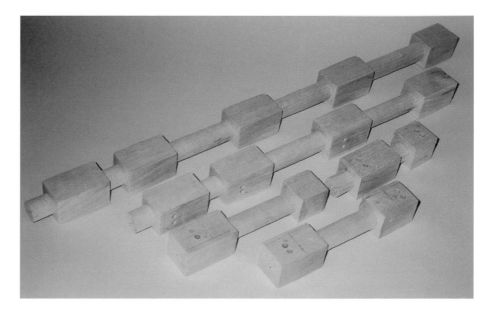

5 The completed lower posts.

Turning the Rear Stretcher

This is made from 5/4 stock, turned to a 1"-diameter cylinder. Starting at the middle, taper the blank to both ends. Turn ½"×¾" stubs on both ends. Sand the piece (see photo 6).

Building the Steps

Use 5/4 stock to make the steps all to the same length of 21½". The top step is somewhat wider than the others to provide a larger platform for a lamp.

To make the shape of the step, first draw a 3" circle (1½" radius) on your stair blank. Then with a beam compass, draw a 20" arc from the center point of that circle. Mark the end points of 9¾" for the wider top step, and 7¾" for the other steps, and then draw lines connecting the smaller 3" circle with those end points.

With a band saw or a saber saw, cut out each of the steps, and smooth all edges. With a Forstner bit, bore a 1" hole in each step, and with your router, round over all the edges with a ½" roundover bit. Sand all parts (see photo 7).

Making the Segments

With the exception of the length, both types of segments are made in the same manner. The table below lists the exact dimensions. Lay out each of the segments, in the quantities specified, and cut out on a band saw or saber saw. Smooth all curves.

Lay out and bore ¼"-diameter holes, ½" deep in all the segments. Sand all parts. Select four of the small segments and designate them #1, #3, #4 and #6. These require countersunk holes to accommodate the #8×1¾" wood screws that will secure the steps during final assembly (see photo 8).

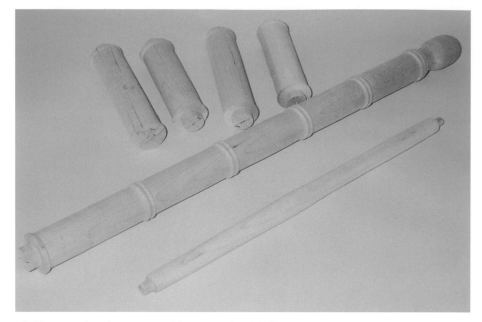

6 The completed rear post with mounted end ball, spacers and stretcher.

7 The completed stair treads. Remember that the top tread is slightly wider to accommodate a lamp.

Segments

SEG	QTY	A	B	C	D	WOOD THICKNESS
Small	6	5⁹⁄₁₆	6	19" radius	18" radius	¾
Large	4	12⅝	13½	19" radius	18" radius	¾

Dimensions in inches

Segment and Post Assembly

Assembly of the segments to the posts requires the use of ¼" dowel centers to locate the ¼" holes in the segment ends to the posts. It is important that the segments be located with their respective post positions in this sequence:

1. Place the dowel centers in one end of small segment #1. Center on the 7⁹⁄₁₆" post and press the segment to the post, thus leaving two indentation marks on the post. Bore two ¼"×½"-deep holes in the post. Using two ¼"× 1" dowels, test fit the segment to the post. Do not glue in any dowels at this time.

2. For segment #2, shift the dowel centers to the other end of the small segment #1 and do the same operation as before for segment #1.

3. Repeat the same operation for small segment #3 to the 18¾" post.

4. Repeat the same operation for small segment #3 to the 7⁹⁄₁₆" post.

5. Repeat the same operation for small segment #3 to the 7⁹⁄₁₆" post and then to the 25" post.

6. Repeat the same operation for small segment #4 to the 7⁹⁄₁₆" post and then to the 18¾" post.

7. Repeat the same operation for large segment #1 to the 18¾" post and then to the 25" post.

8. Repeat the same operation for small segment #6 to the 5¹⁵⁄₁₆" post and then to the 7⁹⁄₁₆" post.

9. Repeat the same operation for small segment #5 to the 7⁹⁄₁₆" post and to the 18¾" post.

10. Repeat the same operation for large segment #2 to the 18¾" post and to the 25" post.

11. Repeat the same operation for large segment #4 to the 5¹⁵⁄₁₆" post and to the 18¾" post.

12. Repeat the same operation for large segment #3 to the 18¾" post and to the 25" post.

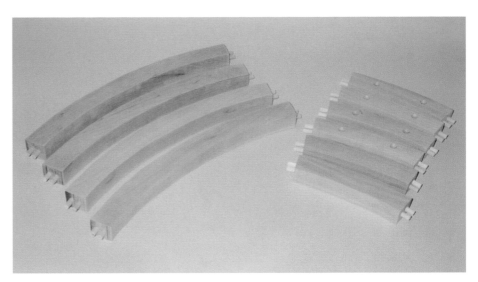

8 The completed segments with attached mounting dowels.

Gluing the Joints

Since there are so many joints to keep track of, it's a good idea to number the joints on the posts and on the segment ends.

Glue the dowels to the segments (two dowels per side). In gluing the segments to the posts, it should be done in a couple of time spans as follows:

1. Glue small segments #1 and #2 to the 7⁹⁄₁₆" and 25" posts respectively. Set aside to dry.

2. Glue small segment #3 and large segments #1, #2 and #3 to the 18¾" post. Set aside to dry.

3. Glue small segments #4 and #5 to the 7⁹⁄₁₆" post. Set aside to dry.

4. Glue small segment #6 and large segment #4 to the 5¹⁵⁄₁₆" post. Set aside to dry.

5. Glue the four segments attached to the 18¾" post to the 7⁹⁄₁₆" post and the 25" post.

6. Small segments #4 and #5 to the 18¾" post.

7. Finally, glue small segment #6 and large segment #4 to the 7⁹⁄₁₆" and 18¾" posts respectively.

Final Assembly

Before final gluing, temporarily assemble the table and mark the locations on the bottom of the steps where the #8× 1¾" wood screws will go. Drill the pilot holes. Begin final assembly by assembling and gluing the bottom spacer to the fourth step as well as gluing the rear stretcher to the 25" post and the bottom spacer. Don't screw down the stairs until all the gluing is finished. Continue assembling and gluing spacers and steps starting from the bottom. Screw each of the steps in place. Finally, glue the upper post in place.

Finishing

Since I used cherry for this project, I chose a clear finish to allow the wood to darken to its own natural beauty. To duplicate this finish, apply one coat of gloss polyurethane and two coats of satin polyurethane. Between coats, lightly sand with 400-grit wet/dry paper, wiping with a tack rag after sanding. Once the finish is dry, apply a good grade of cabinet wax and buff with 0000 steel wool.

Glass-Front Wall Cabinet

This wall-mounted cabinet, made of cherry, is suitable to be used as a kitchen spice cabinet or to hold your favorite collectibles. The design features a simple wall-mounting system. The shelves are made to be removed, and they can be set at various heights.

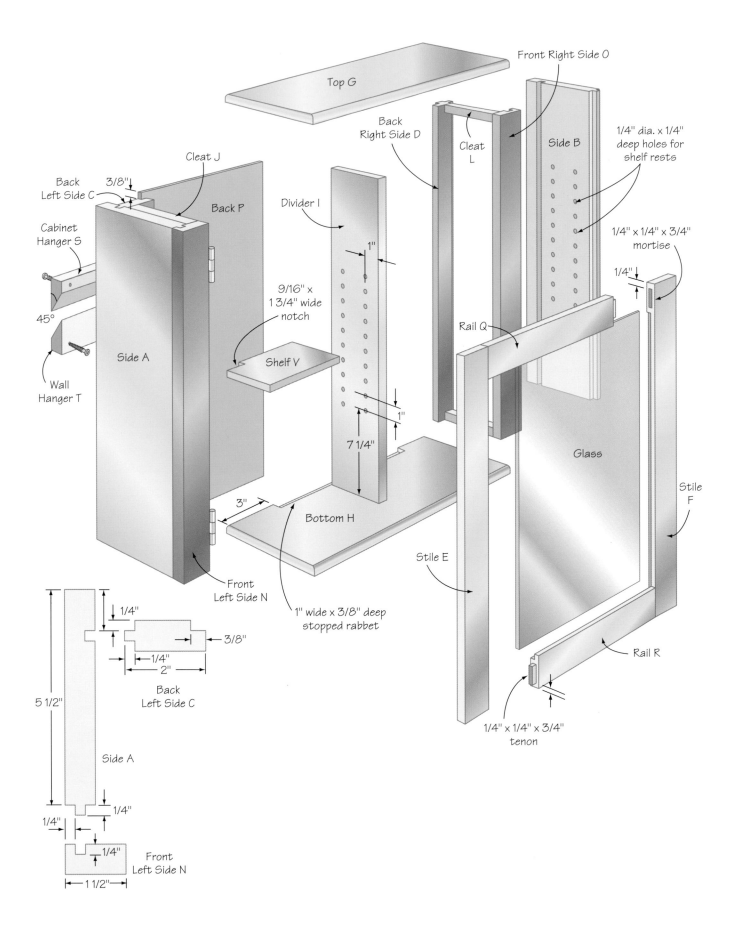

Top G

Front Right Side O

Back Right Side D

Cleat J

Cleat L

Side B

3/8"

Back Left Side C

Back P

Divider I

1/4" dia. x 1/4" deep holes for shelf rests

Cabinet Hanger S

1"

9/16" x 1 3/4" wide notch

1/4" x 1/4" x 3/4" mortise

1/4"

45°

Side A

Shelf V

Rail Q

Wall Hanger T

Glass

1"

7 1/4"

Stile F

3"

Bottom H

Stile E

Front Left Side N

1" wide x 3/8" deep stopped rabbet

Rail R

1/4" x 1/4" x 3/4" tenon

1/4"

3/8"

1/4"

2"

Back Left Side C

5 1/2"

Side A

1/4"

1/4"

1/4"

Front Left Side N

1 1/2"

Cutting List • Glass-Front Wall Cabinet

REF.	QTY.	PART	STOCK	THICK	WIDTH	LENGTH	COMMENTS
A	1	Left Side	Cherry	¾	5½	22½	
B	1	Right Side	Cherry	¾	5½	22½	
C	1	Left Back	Cherry	¾	2	22½	
D	1	Right Back	Cherry	¾	2	22½	
E	1	Left Door Stile	Cherry	¾	1½	22⁷⁄₁₆	
F	1	Right Door Stile	Cherry	¾	1½	22⁷⁄₁₆	
G	1	Top	Cherry	¾	6¾	20	
H	1	Bottom	Cherry	¾	6¾	20	
I	1	Divider	Cherry	¾	3¾	22½	
J, K, L, M	4	Cleats	Cherry	¾	¾	3⅝	
N	1	Left Front	Cherry	¾	1½	22½	
O	1	Right Front	Cherry	¾	1½	22½	
P	1	Back (Plywood)	Plywood	¼	14¹³⁄₁₆	23¼	
Q	1	Top Door Rail	Cherry	¾	1½	22½	
R	1	Bottom Door Rail	Cherry	¾	1½	12¹⁵⁄₁₆	
S, T	1	Hanger Assembly	Cherry	¾	2½	17	
U	2	Left Shelves	Cherry	¾	4⅛	8	
V	2	Right Shelves	Cherry	¾	4⅛	8	

Hardware

1	⅛ x 13 x 19¹⁵⁄₁₆ Glass Sheet
1	Knob (Rockler #35832)
0	Tapered Pads (Rockler #28530)
2	2" x 1⅜" Hinges (Stanley #80-3240)
1	Cabinet Catch (Stanley #71-1030)
6	Shelf Hangers (Woodcraft #27114)
6	#6 x 1¼" Flathead Screws
4	#6 x 2" Flathead Screws

Supplies

Carpenter's Glue
Gloss Polyurethane
Satin Polyurethane
#400 Wet/Dry Paper

REQUIRED TOOLS

Table or circular saw

Drill or drill press

Router

Mortise chisel

Sander (or sandpaper and block)

Left and Right Side Assembly

Cut parts A, B, C, D, N and O to the overall sizes as listed in the bill of materials. Using a dado attachment on your table saw, cut $\frac{1}{4}" \times \frac{1}{4}"$ dadoes in parts A, B, N and O. Then cut matching tenons in parts A, B, C and D, making sure they fit snugly into their respective dadoes. Parts C and D each have a $\frac{1}{4}" \times \frac{3}{8}"$ rabbet cut into the back side.

Side Assembly

Glue and clamp parts N and C to side A, and parts D and O to side B.

Cleat Assembly

Cut cleats J, K, L and M. Lay out, drill and countersink clearance holes for #6 $\times$ 1$\frac{1}{4}"$ flathead wood screws, (each cleat will have four holes). Sand these and individually fit them to their respective locations. Glue and screw each cleat to the respective side.

Building the Top and Bottom

The same method is used for both G and H. Cut the parts to the overall dimensions as listed on the bill of materials. Using a router, rout a $1" \times \frac{3}{8}"$ deep stopped rabbet on the rear of each piece. Round over the side and front edges of both boards with a $\frac{1}{2}"$ roundover bit. You will notice that there are two screw holes indicated on both boards. These are necessary to secure the divider panel. Drill these holes $2\frac{1}{4}"$ and $4\frac{1}{4}"$ respectively from the back and equidistant from the sides.

Making the Divider

Cut part I to size. Lay out and bore twenty $\frac{1}{4}"$ through holes. These holes are used to hold the shelf-mounting brackets, as shown in the technical drawing.

Side Assemblies

As was done on the divider, lay out and bore twenty $\frac{1}{4}" \times \frac{1}{4}"$-deep holes in each of the side assemblies. It is important that these holes mirror the positions of the respective holes in the divider, or the shelves, when installed, will appear crooked.

Cabinet Assembly

The sides are secured to both the top and bottom with #6$\times$1$\frac{1}{4}"$ flathead wood screws. These screws are inserted through the previously drilled holes in the cleats and screwed into the top and bottom. Position both sides $\frac{3}{4}"$ from the side edges of the top or bottom and flush with the back. Mark the location of the screw holes in the top and bottom and drill pilot holes. Screw the sides to the top and bottom.

Insert the divider, making sure it is centered from left to right and that it backs up to the inner edge of the stopped rabbet on both the top and bottom. Insert #6$\times$2$"$ screws in the holes previously drilled in both the top and bottom. Mark the screw holes and drill pilot holes. Screw the divider to the top and bottom.

Making the Back

Although the dimensions for the back, P, are specified in the cutting list, your version may vary slightly. Therefore, it's better to measure the back opening now than to be sorry later. Cut the $\frac{1}{4}"$ plywood to the correct dimensions and glue and nail it in place with $\frac{5}{8}"$ brads.

Shelf Assembly

Cut the shelves, U and V, to size and check for a proper fit in the cabinet.

Hanger Assembly

The hanger assembly consists of two parts, S, and T, made from $2\frac{1}{2}" \times 17"$ stock, cut as shown in the technical drawing at a 45° angle. Part S is glued and screwed to the cabinet. Part T will be screwed to the wall when the cabinet is installed. You will notice that the two holes in T are spaced 16" apart. The reason for this is that the studs in most house construction are spaced 16" on center, and therefore the hanger assembly can be screwed into two adjoining studs for maximum strength.

Door Assembly

This assembly consists of parts E, F, Q and R. Cut all parts to their overall sizes. Lay out and cut $\frac{1}{4}" \times \frac{3}{4}"$ tenons on each end of Q and R. Mortises to fit the

tenons must now be cut into parts E and F. Using a router with a $\frac{3}{8}"$ straight bit, cut a $\frac{5}{16}" \times \frac{1}{4}"$-deep rabbet into the rear of Q and R. Rout a $\frac{5}{16}" \times \frac{1}{4}"$-deep stopped rabbet in parts E and F. Sand all the parts and glue and clamp them. After the glue has dried, rout the inner front edge of the door assembly with a $\frac{1}{4}"$ beading bit.

Door Installation

It is entirely possible that the door has to be trimmed for a proper fit to the opening of the cabinet. Ideally there should be at least a $\frac{1}{32}"$ clearance around the door and the cabinet. Mortise in the hinges on the cabinet, starting the mortises 3" from the top and bottom respectively. Lay the door in the opening and transfer the mortise dimensions to the door edge. Mortise the hinges into the door. Screw the hinges to the cabinet and then to the door. Check for proper door closure. Disassemble the door and hinges and set them aside until final assembly.

Glass Installation

To install the glass use the tapered pads specified in the materials list. These pads, screwed into the back of the door, will hold the glass in place gently but firmly. Install two on the top, two on the bottom, and three on either side. Remove the pads and glass and set them aside until final assembly. Finally, drill the mounting hole for the knob on the right side of the door.

Finishing

To allow the cherry to darken to its own natural color over a period of time, do not apply any stain. Rather, apply one coat of gloss polyurethane followed by two coats of satin polyurethane. Lightly sand the finish between coats with 400-grit wet/dry paper, and wipe with a tack rag.

Final Assembly

Using the retaining pads, mount the pane of glass to the door, and install the knob. Screw the hinges to the door and then to the cabinet. Install the magnetic cabinet catch and install the four shelves.

Common Adhesives

ADHESIVE	ADVANTAGES	DISADVANTAGES	COMMON USES	WORKING TIME	CLAMPING TIME (at 70° F)	CURE TIME	SOLVENT
Yellow glue (aliphatic resin)	Easy to use; water resistant; water cleanup; economical.	Not waterproof (don't use on outdoor furniture).	All-purpose wood glue for interior use; stronger bond than white glue.	5 to 7 minutes	1 to 2 hours	24 hours	Warm water
Contact cement	Bonds parts immediately.	Can't readjust parts after contact.	Bonding wood veneer or plastic laminate to substrate.	Up to 1 hour	No clamps; parts bond on contact	–	Acetone
Super glue (Cyanoacrylate)	Bonds parts quickly.	Limited to small parts.	Bonding small parts made from a variety of materials.	30 seconds	10 to 60 seconds; clamps usually not required	30 minutes to several hours	Acetone
Epoxy glue	Good gap filler; waterproof; fast setting formulas available; can be used to bond glass to metal or wood.	Requires mixing.	Bonding small parts made from a variety of materials.	5 to 60 minutes depending on epoxy formula	5 minutes to several hours depending on epoxy formula	3 hours and longer	Lacquer thinner
Animal glue, dry (hide glue)	Extended working time; water cleanup; economical.	Must be mixed with water and heated; poor moisture resistance (don't use on outdoor furniture).	Time-consuming assembly work; stronger bond than liquid animal glue; interior use only.	30 minutes	2 to 3 hours	24 hours	Warm water
Animal glue, liquid (hide glue)	Easy to use; extended working time; water cleanup; economical.	Poor moisture resistance (don't use on outdoor furniture).	Time-consuming assembly work; interior use only.	5 minutes	2 hours	24 hours	Warm water
Polyurethane	Fully waterproof; gap-filling.	Eye and skin irritant.	Multi-purpose, interior and exterior applications including wood to wood, ceramic, plastic, Corian, stone, metal.	30 minutes	1 to 2 hours	8 hours	Mineral spirits while wet; must abrade or scrape off when dry.
White glue (polyvinyl acetate)	Easy to use; economical.	Not waterproof (don't use on outdoor furniture).	All-purpose wood glue for interior use; yellow glue has stronger bond.	3 to 5 minutes	16 hours	24 to 48 hours	Warm water and soap
Waterproof glue (resorcinol)	Fully waterproof; extended working time.	Requires mixing; dark color shows glue line on most woods; long clamping time.	Outdoor furniture, marine applications.	20 minutes	1 hour	12 hours	Cool water before hardening
Plastic resin (urea formaldehyde)	Good water resistance; economical.	Requires mixing; long clamping time.	Outdoor furniture, cutting boards.	15 to 30 minutes	6 hours	24 hours	Warm water and soap before hardening

Wine Rack

This wine rack will hold 16 bottles of wine. The bottles will lie in the rack and be tilted so that the corks in the bottles will stay moist and not dry out. The rack can either be placed on the floor, or rest on a shelf. I used cherry for this project, but any species of wood would be appropriate.

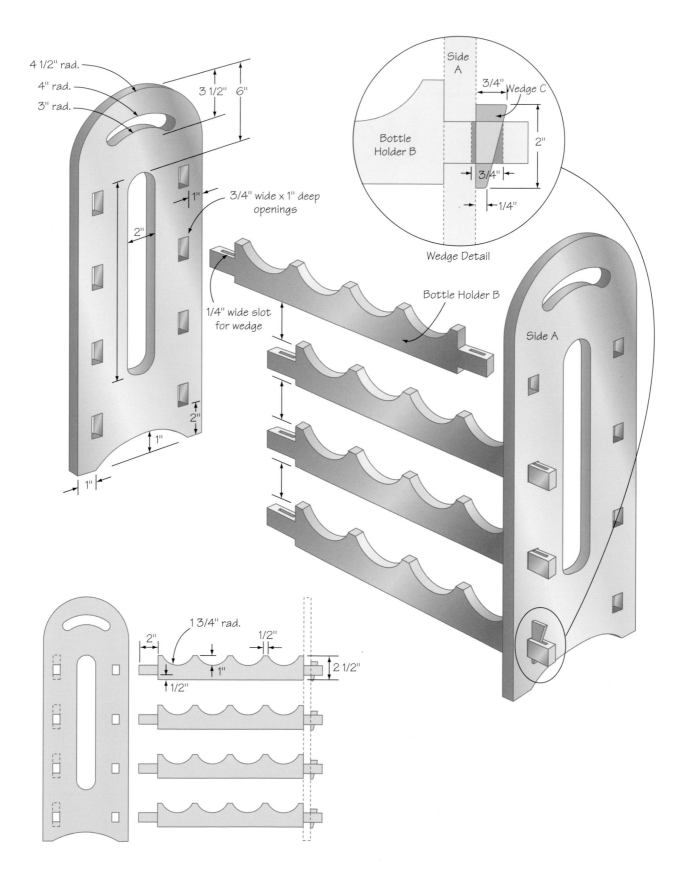

4 1/2" rad.

4" rad.

3" rad.

3 1/2" 6"

1"

2"

3/4" wide x 1" deep openings

2"

1/4" wide slot for wedge

2"

1"

1"

Side A

3/4"

Wedge C

Bottle Holder B

2"

3/4"

1/4"

Wedge Detail

Bottle Holder B

Side A

1 3/4" rad.

2"

1/2"

1/2"

1"

2 1/2"

Cutting List • Wine Rack

REF.	QTY.	PART	STOCK	THICK	WIDTH	LENGTH	COMMENTS
A	2	Sides	Cherry	¾	9	25	
B	8	Bottle Holders	Cherry	¾	2½	19⁄₁₆	
C	6	Wedges	Cherry	¼	¾	2	

Supplies

	Gloss Polyurethane
	Satin Polyurethane
	#400 Wet/Dry Paper

Making the Sides

Cut out the sides to the dimensions listed in the cutting list. Lay out all the dimensions shown in the technical drawing. Eight through mortises have to be cut in each side. Do this first. If you have a drill press and a ¾" Forstner bit, bore a hole exactly in the center of each of the eight mortise locations. Square up the holes using a wood chisel and a mallet. When doing this operation, make sure there is a wooden backing board beneath to preclude any breakout on the down side, away from the chisel.

Bore out the ends of the handholds with a 1" Forstner bit, and the ends of the slots with a 2" Forstner bit. Cut out the vertical slot in each of the sides with a saber saw or a coping saw. Smooth each of the slot sides using a spokeshave. Blend the sides into the circular ends with a file. The hand holds can be cut out using either a saber saw or a coping saw. Smooth the slots with files. With a ¼" roundover bit in your router, round over all outer edges of the sides, the vertical slots and the handholds. Sand all surfaces of the sides.

Making the Bottle Holders

Cut the eight holders to the overall size of 2½"×19⁄₁₆". Either lay out the measurements on each of the eight holders, or make a template from a ¼" piece of plywood and transfer the shape to each holder. All the cutting on the holders can be done using a band saw or, if one is not available, a coping saw. Use a back saw to cut the end tenons. File and sand smooth all curved surfaces.

The end tenons have to be sized to fit the mortises in the side pieces. This can be accomplished using straight chisels and files. With a ¼" roundover bit in your router, round over all surfaces (but not the end tenons). On each of the end tenons lay out the dimensions for a mortise ¼"×¼"×¾" long to accept the wedges. Bore out the mortise slots using a ¼" bit, and square up each slot with a wood chisel. Sand each holder.

Cutting the Wedges

This project requires 16 wedges made from ¼" stock, sized to a dimension of ¾"×2". Cut the slanted edge of each wedge and smooth all edges. Make sure that the wedges will fit the mortises in the holders.

Assembly

Assemble the project as shown in the technical drawing. Tap the wedges in place. They should fit fairly easily. If this is not the case, trim the individual wedges to fit. When fully assembled the wine rack should present a sturdy platform for your collection of wine bottles.

Finishing

Finishing this project is really quite simple. Since cherry was used, no stain need be applied. Apply one coat of gloss polyurethane. Follow this with two coats of satin polyurethane. Between coats sand lightly with 400-grit wet/dry paper.

REQUIRED TOOLS

Table or circular saw

Drill or drill press

Chisels

Mallet

Saber saw or coping saw

Spokeshave

File

Sander (or sandpaper and block)

Back saw

Bookrack Table

Placed beside a sofa or easy chair, this little table, made from walnut, provides a fine platform for a lamp, as well as a convenient bookrack to hold your favorite novels.

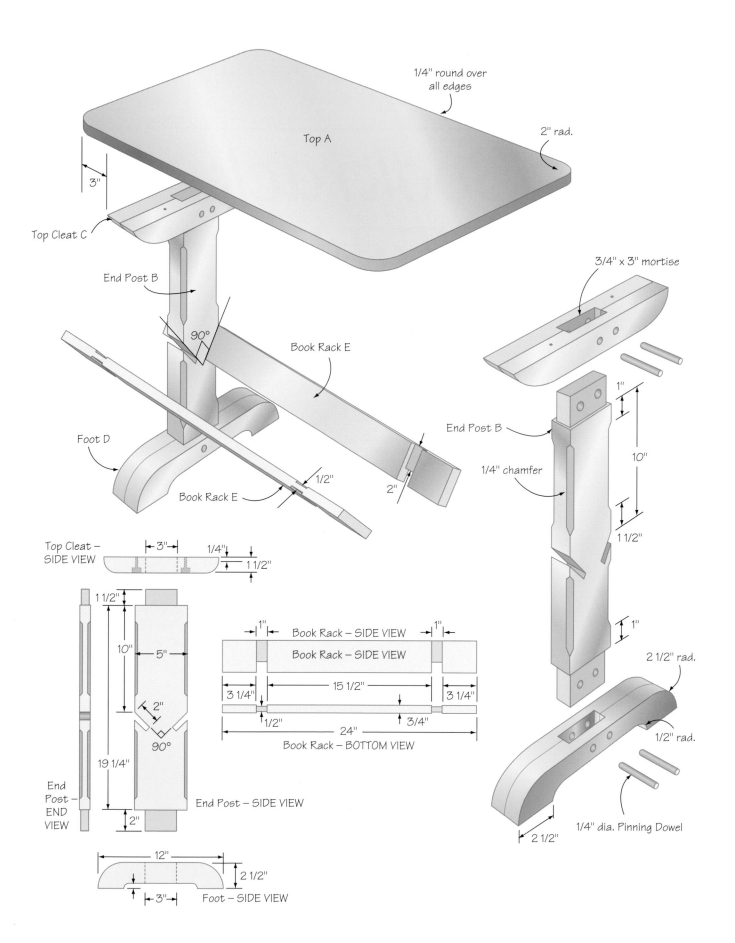

1/4" round over all edges

Top A

2" rad.

3"

Top Cleat C

End Post B

90°

Book Rack E

Foot D

Book Rack E

1/2"

2"

3/4" x 3" mortise

End Post B

1/4" chamfer

1"

10"

1 1/2"

1"

2 1/2" rad.

1/2" rad.

1/4" dia. Pinning Dowel

2 1/2"

Top Cleat – SIDE VIEW

3"

1/4"

1 1/2"

1 1/2"

10"

5"

2"

90°

19 1/4"

End Post – END VIEW

End Post – SIDE VIEW

2"

Book Rack – SIDE VIEW

1"

Book Rack – SIDE VIEW

1"

15 1/2"

3 1/4"

3 1/4"

1/2"

3/4"

24"

Book Rack – BOTTOM VIEW

12"

2 1/2"

3"

Foot – SIDE VIEW

Cutting List • Bookrack Table

REF.	QTY.	PART	STOCK	THICK	WIDTH	LENGTH	COMMENTS
A	1	Top	4/4 Walnut	3/4	12	24	Glued-up dimensions
B	2	End Posts	5/4 Walnut	1	5	22¾	
C	2	Top Cleats	4/4 Walnut	1½	1½	11	Glued-up dimensions
D	2	Feet	4/4 Walnut	1½	2½	12	Glued-up dimensions
E	2	Book Racks	Walnut	3/4	3	24	

Hardware

	8	¼ x 1½ Pinning Dowels
	4	#8 x 1¾ Wood Screws

Supplies

	Carpenter's Glue
	Walnut Stain
	Clear Tung Oil Varnish
	#600 Wet/Dry Paper
	Cabinet Wax

Making the Top Cleats
Make the cleats by laminating two pieces of 4/4 walnut stock and shaping them as shown in the technical drawing. Before gluing them up, lay out and cut a ⅜"×3" dado slot in each of the matching pieces (it's easier to do this then to chop out a mortise after lamination). Cut and shape the ends, and rout a ¼" roundover as indicated in the technical drawing. Bore two ⅜"×¼"-deep holes, and drill oversized clearance holes for the #8×1¾" mounting screws in both of the cleats.

Making the Feet
Similar to the cleats, make the feet by laminating two pieces of 4/4 stock and shaping as shown in the technical drawing. Again, before laminating, cut the dadoes.

Making the End Posts
Make the end posts from two 5/4 pieces of 5"×22¾" walnut. Before doing any cutting, lay out all dimensions. The two slots for the bookracks are situated 90° to each other. Cut the two end tenons and, with a band saw or a saber saw, cut the bookrack slots. Fit the tenons to the mortises in the top cleats and feet. Cut ¼" chamfers in each of the end posts (although the chamfers aren't necessary, they add to the attractiveness of the project).

Making the Bookracks
Cut the two pieces to the overall size listed in the cutting list, and using a dado set, cut the two dado slots. Notch each of the slots as shown, and trim and fit these pieces to their respective slots in the end posts. Rout a ¼" roundover on all outer edges.

Making the Top
Joint, glue and clamp enough 4/4 walnut stock to make a 12"×24" blank. After the glue has dried, size to the proper dimensions. Cut a 2" radius on each of the four corners. Rout a ¼" roundover on the top and bottom edges.

End Post Assembly
Dry assemble the feet and top cleats to the end posts. Lay out and bore two ¼"×1½"-deep stopped holes in the feet and cleats respectively (these holes will be used for the pinning dowels). Cut eight 1½" pinning dowels from ¼" dowel stock. Glue the cleats and feet to the posts. Glue and insert the dowels.

Final Assembly
Glue both bookracks to the end posts. Place this subassembly on the bottom side of the top, and center it. Mark the four mounting screw holes, and drill four stopped pilot holes in the top (make sure you don't drill completely through the top surface). Finally, screw the end post assemblies to the top.

Finishing
With a rag, apply two coats of walnut stain, followed by three coats of clear tung oil varnish. Allow the finish to dry for at least eight hours before applying the next coat. Sand lightly with 600-grit wet/dry sandpaper between coats of the tung oil. Wipe the assembly between coats with a tack rag. Each successive coat will be absorbed less and less until the film is built up to the surface. After the finish is thoroughly dry, apply a coat of cabinet wax and buff to a high sheen.

REQUIRED TOOLS

- Jointer
- Table saw or circular saw
- Clamps
- Router
- Drill or drill press
- Sander (or sandpaper and block)

Drawer Bookcase

This little beauty will be at home in any room. Not only will it hold books, but there's a drawer for all of the small stuff. It is made from cherry, although any wood is appropriate, and finished with a few coats of tung oil varnish.

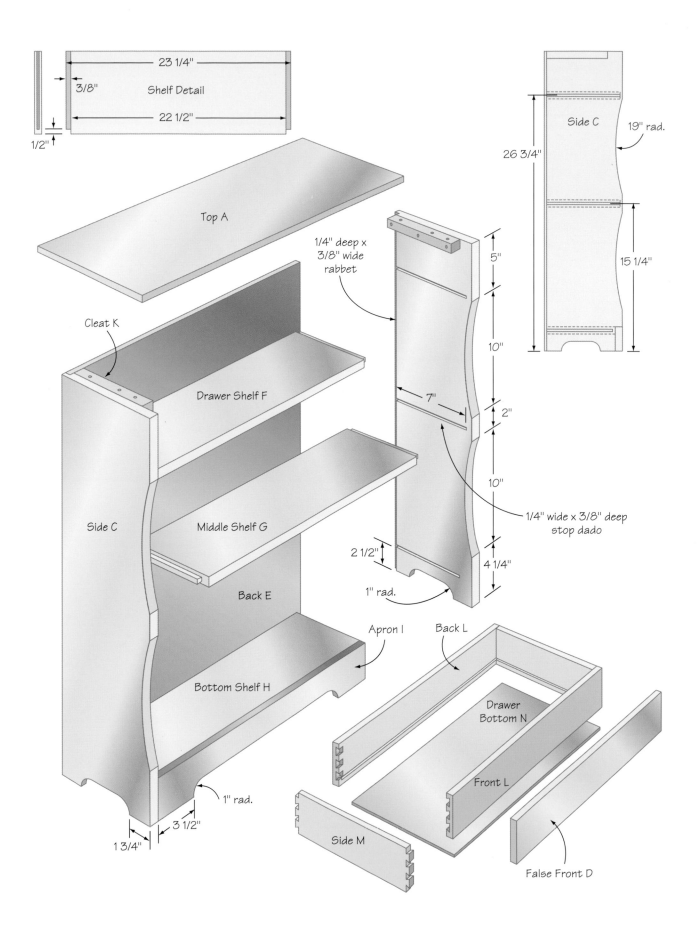

23 1/4"

3/8"   Shelf Detail

22 1/2"

1/2"

Top A

1/4" deep x 3/8" wide rabbet

Side C

19" rad.

26 3/4"

5"

10"

15 1/4"

Cleat K

Drawer Shelf F

7"

2"

Side C

Middle Shelf G

10"

1/4" wide x 3/8" deep stop dado

Back E

2 1/2"

4 1/4"

1" rad.

Bottom Shelf H

Apron I

Back L

Drawer Bottom N

Front L

Side M

False Front D

1" rad.

3 1/2"

1 3/4"

Cutting List • Drawer Bookcase

REF.	QTY.	PART	STOCK	THICK	WIDTH	LENGTH	COMMENTS
A	1	Top	Cherry	¾	8¾	28	
B	1	Side	Cherry	¾	8	31¼	
C	1	Side	Cherry	¾	8	31¼	
D	1	False Front	Cherry	¾	4⅛	22⅜	
E	1	Back	Cherry	¼	23¼	29½	Tailor to fit opening
F	1	Drawer Shelf	Cherry	¾	7¾	23¼	
G	1	Middle Shelf	Cherry	¾	7¾	23¼	
H	1	Bottom Shelf	Cherry	¾	7	24¼	
I	1	Apron	Cherry	¾	3	22½	
K	2	Side Cleats	Cherry	¾	¾	6¼	
L	2	Drawer Front & Back	Cherry	½	2¾	22⅜	
M	2	Drawer Sides	Cherry	½	2¾	6½	
N	1	Drawer Bottom	Cherry	¼	6⅜	21⅞	

Hardware

	2	1¼" White Porcelain Knobs
	12	#6 x 1¼" Flathead Wood Screws

Supplies

Carpenter's Glue

Tung Oil Varnish

#400 Wet/Dry Paper

Drawer Tape (Rockler's #70615)

REQUIRED TOOLS

Table or circular saw

Jointer

Router

Jig saw, saber saw or band saw

Sander (or sandpaper and block)

Chisel

Dovetail jig

Making the Sides

Cut and joint enough wood to make two panels with the dimensions as listed in the cutting list. Lay out the dimension lines shown in the technical drawing (i.e., the 19" radii, the bottom cutouts and the three slots). Set up your router with a ¼" straight bit and set the depth to ⅜". Rout the three stopped slots in each side. Using a saber saw or a band saw, cut out the 19" radii on the sides and the bottom openings. Sand smooth all the curved surfaces. Cut a ¼" × ⅜" rabbet on the back edge of each board, either by using the router with the same ¼" straight bit in the previous operation or by using a table saw with a dado blade. Finish sand each side.

Building the Shelves

Cut and joint enough wood to make the three shelves to the dimensions listed in the cutting list. Set up and cut the ¼" dadoes. It's possible to do this on the table saw with either a dado set or by multiple passes with a regular blade. This can also be done on a radial arm saw. Make sure that the resulting dadoes fit comfortably into the slots previously cut in the sides. When doing this, it is a good idea to sneak up on the final ¼" dado dimension with a cut and try operation. Sand each of the shelves.

Making the Apron

Cut the apron to the dimensions listed in the bill of materials. Lay out and cut the bottom edge with either a saber saw or a band saw. Sand this edge smooth, then sand the entire apron.

Assembling the Apron

Glue and clamp the apron to the front edge of the bottom shelf. Make sure that the apron fits exactly to the 22½" dimension of the bottom shelf.

Making the Cleats

Cut out the two ¾" × 6¼" cleats to the dimensions listed in the bill of materi-als. Mark and bore six clearance holes for #6 × 1¼" flathead wood screws. During the assembly process, these cleats will be screwed and glued to the top.

Making the Top

Cut and joint the top to the dimensions listed in the cutting list. Sand the top smooth. Round over the upper and lower edges of the front and sides with a ¼" roundover router bit. A ¼" × ⅜" stopped rabbet has to be cut into the back edge of the top. This can best be done after the proper dimension is determined during dry assembly.

Assembling the Carcass

Dry assemble and clamp the sides to the shelves. This step is necessary in order to check the fit of the shelves into the side slots, to determine where the two cleats are to be screwed to the top, to determine where the pilot holes will be drilled into the sides, and to determine the dimensions to stop the ⅜" rabbet. While the assembly is clamped together, the final dimensions of the back can also be determined. When finally installed, the back will tend to keep the entire assembly in square.

Rout the ⅜" rabbet into the rear edge of the top. At the stopped ends, square off the rounded portions with a chisel. Glue and screw the two cleats to the top in the positions determined during dry assembly. Glue and clamp the shelves to the sides. When doing this operation, clamp the assembly with the front face down to enable the assembly of the back to the rest of the carcass. Fit the top to the assembly and screw the cleats to the sides. Glue and tack the back to the assembly with ⅝" brads. If all went well, the assembly will be in square.

Drawer Construction

Cut the false front to the dimensions listed in the bill of materials. Determine where the two knobs are to be located, and drill the pilot holes for the knob screws. It's a good idea to counterbore the rear portion of these holes ⅛" deep to accept the screw heads, thus allowing the false front to fit correctly to the drawer front when the six mounting screws are applied. Round over all the edges with a ¼" roundover router bit. Sand the false front. Cut the sides, front and back to the correct sizes.

This project as described has dovetail joints joining the four sides of the drawer assembly. These joints were made using a dovetail jig. There are many such jigs on the market, or if you like, you can cut your dovetails by hand. Whichever method you use, cut the dovetails so that the joints fit tight. Cut ¼" × ¼" dadoes ¼" up from the inside edge of all four sides of the drawer assembly, parts L and M. The drawer bottom will fit in this slot. Cut the bottom to the dimensions listed in the bill of materials. To ensure a proper cut, dry assemble the four sides and measure the openings for the bottom. Round over all the edges of the four sides. Glue and assemble the drawer. Don't screw the false front to the drawer assembly at this time.

Finishing

Since cherry was the wood of choice, no stain was used. This allows the wood to naturally darken to its own beautiful color over a period of about a year. Thoroughly remove any sanding dust from the project using a tack rag. With a lint-free rag, apply six or seven coats of tung oil varnish to the project. Apply only one coat per day. After the second coat, and each suceeding coat thereafter, sand lightly with 400 grit wet/dry paper and wipe with a tack rag.

Final Assembly

Screw the two knobs to the false front. Screw the false front to the drawer assembly. To obtain a smooth-sliding drawer, apply a couple pieces of drawer tape to the inside edges of the drawer compartment (where the edge of the drawer will rest on the drawer compartment).

HAND-CUTTING DOVETAILS

Half-blind dovetails work well on drawers when you want to see the front without jointery showing. Cutting them is a little more difficult than cutting regular through-dovetails. It's better to cut the tails first so they can be used to layout the mortises on the front.

Begin by setting your marking gauge to two-thirds the thickness of the drawer front and scribe the shoulder lines for the side on both of the side pieces. Use a T- bevel gauge set to a 1:8 pitch or about $7\frac{1}{2}°$ to layout the tails on the side. Mark the waste in between the tails in pencil.

With the side held in a vise, make the vertical cuts on the waste side of the lines using a dovetail saw or small back saw. Stop your cuts just shy of the shoulder marks. Cut out the waste between the tails with a coping saw. Carefully trim to the lines using a sharp chisel.

Reset your marking gauge to the thickness of the sides. Scribe the shoulder line for the side on the inside of the drawer front. Lay the drawer side on the end of the front and scribe the tails onto the front. Mark the waste in pencil and use a sharp

chisel to cut out the waste areas. Carefully cut just to the lines. Dry fit the side into the front. It should be a snug fit using a block of wood and a hammer to put the pieces together. Use a light touch to pare away the tightly fitting sections if needed.

The back of the drawer and the sides may be joined using through-dovetails. Layout for these dovetails can be done in the reverse order of half-blind layout. Start by scribing a shoulder line the thickness of the side onto the back. Layout the tails on the end of the back at the 1:8 pitch. Mark the right angle lines connecting the beveled lines with the shoulder scribe using a square. Mark these lines on both sides of the back pieces so you can see the proper angle to make the saw cuts. Make the vertical cuts with a backsaw and trim the waste with a coping saw. Trim carefully to the lines using a chisel.

Scribe a shoulder line on the side the same thickness as the back. Then stand the back up on end on the side using the shoulder scribe to line up the back. Trace the pins onto the side. Mark the waste and cut as before. Trim to the lines and fit as described above.

Trestle Table

This rustic table is a natural for a family that has lots of kids and a large dining area. The tabletop allows ample room for plates, silverware and servers. Made from red oak, stained and given a polyurethane finish, it will be a durable, fine piece of furniture.

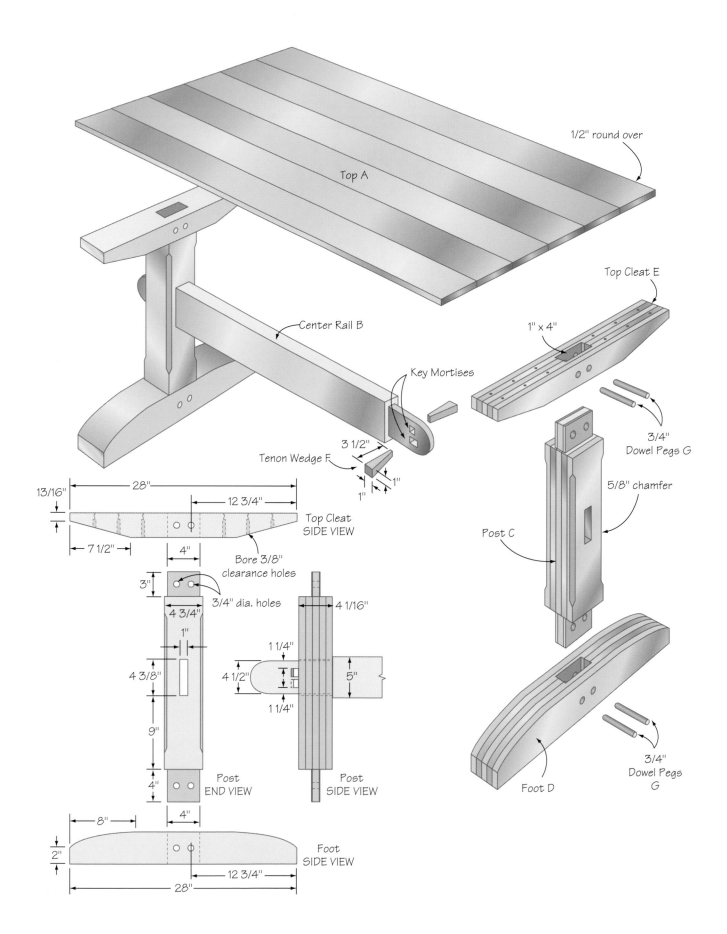

1/2" round over

Top A

Top Cleat E

1" x 4"

Center Rail B

Key Mortises

3/4"
Dowel Pegs G

5/8" chamfer

Post C

3 1/2"

Tenon Wedge F

1"

1"

13/16"

28"

12 3/4"

Top Cleat
SIDE VIEW

7 1/2"

4"

Bore 3/8"
clearance holes

3"

4 3/4"

3/4" dia. holes

4 1/16"

1"

1 1/4"

4 3/8"

4 1/2"

5"

9"

1 1/4"

4"

Post
END VIEW

Post
SIDE VIEW

Foot D

3/4"
Dowel Pegs
G

8"

4"

2"

Foot
SIDE VIEW

12 3/4"

28"

Cutting List • Trestle Table

REF.	QTY.	PART	STOCK	THICK	WIDTH	LENGTH	COMMENTS
A	1	Top	8/4 Oak	1¾	40	76	Glued-up dimensions
B	1	Center Rail	8/4 Oak	1¾	5	63½	
C	2	Posts	4/4 Oak	4	4¾	28	Glued-up dimensions
D	2	Feet	4/4 Oak	4	4	28	Glued-up dimensions
E	2	Cleats	4/4 Oak	4	3	28	Glued-up dimensions
F	4	Wedges	Oak	1	1	3½	
G	8	Pegs	Oak	¾ Dia.		4 1/16	

Hardware

	24	#8 x 2" Flathead Screws

Supplies

- Carpenter's Glue
- Old Masters #40101 Natural Stain
- Old Masters #40601 Maple Stain
- Old Masters #49408 Gloss Polyurethane
- Old Masters Satin Polyurethane
- #600 Wet/Dry Paper

Required Tools

- Jointer
- Clamps
- Hand plane
- Sander (or sandpaper and block)
- Length of pipe
- Table saw
- Band saw
- Drill
- Chisels

Building the Top

Make the top by edge gluing six or seven ¾ boards that you've either edge-jointed on a jointer or with a hand jointer plane. Glue and clamp the top assembly, either a few boards at a time or all at once. Due to the thickness of the top boards and the length, I recommend gluing the boards a couple at a time. After the glue has dried, hand plane and sand both the top and bottom surfaces flat. In order to determine the high and low spots on both surfaces, roll a length of pipe over the surface and look for light between the wood and pipe. Round over all top and bottom edges with a ½" router bit.

Making the Top Cleats

Make the top cleats by laminating ¼ stock. Instead of chopping out the mortises after the boards are glued up, form the rough mortise before gluing up the cleat assemblies. To do so, cut the middle boards to a 12" length and put a slight dado into the neighboring boards so that the resulting rough opening measures 1"×4".

After the glue has dried, trace the shape of the top cleat on the blanks. Cut the cleats to shape with a band saw. Sand the cleats smooth. If one is available, an oscillating spindle sander works well for this task.

Using a ⅜" Forstner bit, counterbore twelve clearance holes to accommodate the heads of the 2" wood screws. The depth of each hole is bored so that there is 1" of wood remaining. To accomodate the seasonal shrinking and swelling of wood, drill an oversized clearance hole in the center of each screw hole for the bodies of the #8×2" wood screws.

Making the Feet

Use the same method to make the feet that you used to fabricate the cleats. Sand the feet smooth.

Making the Posts

Each post is made by laminating five pieces of 4"×28" ¼ stock. After the glue has dried, lay out the dimensions for the end tenons, the side chamfers and

1 Here is the completed assembly of the top cleat, post and foot. Notice the doweling in both the top cleat and the foot.

center rail mortise. Cut the tenons to size and then chop out the mortise. This operation can be accomplished by roughing the mortise out with a 1" Forstner bit. Square up the mortise sides and ends with mortising chisels, smoothing the inside of each mortise to the approximate 1"×4" dimension. Lay out and cut the four chamfers on the posts, and sand the posts smooth. Choose a foot and a cleat for each post, and fit the tenons to each of the mortises by trimming each tenon with a chisel until it fits snugly.

Assembly of Post to Top Cleat and Foot

Layout the location of the wooden pegs on both the cleats and feet as seen in the technical drawing. Fit the post to the top cleat and bore two ¾" holes through the assembly with a ¾" Forstner bit. Do the same thing with the post and foot assembly. The wooden pegs can be made from commonly available ¾" hardwood doweling, or oak dowels can be turned on a lathe. Apply glue to the dowel holes and tap the dowel pegs in place using a mallet or

hammer and a protective piece of wood (see photo 1).

Making the Center Rail

Cut the center rail to the overall length as shown in the cutting list. Lay out and cut the two end tenons and fit them to their respective mortises on the posts. See the technical drawing for the location of the four mortises that must be cut to accommodate the wedges. Layout and cut these mortises.

Make four wedges from scrap pieces of oak. Trim the wedges to fit the mortises in the center rail. Cut a radius of 2½" on each end of the center rail, and sand the ends smooth. Round over the four long edges of the center rail with a ½" roundover bit. Sand the entire surface of the rail.

Assembly of Center Rail to Post Assemblies

Fit the ends of the center rail into the mortises in the post assemblies. Insert the four wedges and lightly tap them home with a wooden mallet. The result of this assembly will be a very sturdy platform (see photos 2 and 3).

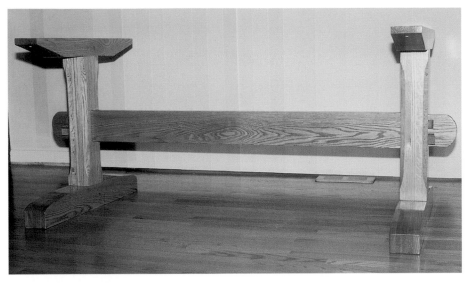

2 Here you see the center rail mounted in the post assemblies.

Assembly of Top to Platform

Invert the top on your bench. Place the post assembly, top side down, on the tabletop. Center the post assembly on the top. Place the screws in the holes in the top cleats and mark each of the screw positions. Drill pilot holes for the screws, making sure not to drill through the top. Screw the post assembly to the top.

Finishing

Since this project is made from beautiful red oak, I wanted the grain to be highlighted in the finished project. I wiped on a coat of stain that I mixed from three parts of Old Masters Natural #40101 stain and one part of Old Masters Maple #40601 finishing stain. After the stain had dried, I applied one coat of Old Masters #49408 gloss polyurethane, followed by two coats of Old Masters satin polyurethane. Between coats I lightly sanded with 600-grit wet/dry paper and removed all sanding particles with a tack rag.

3 Detail of the wedges used to secure the center rail to the post assemblies.

Ladder-Back Chair

This attractive, ladder-back chair is made from cherry. The lathe turnings and the colorful woven seat will blend into any setting. Although the chair in this project was given a water-soluble aniline stain, the wood could have been left a natural color and the chair would be equally appealing.

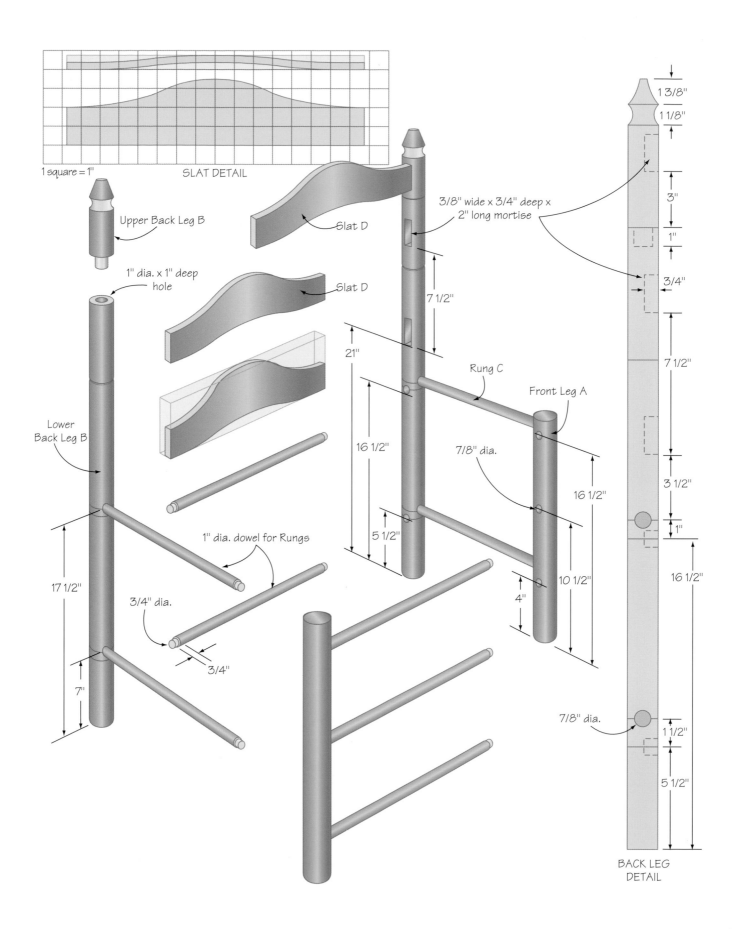

SLAT DETAIL

1 square = 1"

Upper Back Leg B

1" dia. x 1" deep hole

Slat D

Slat D

Lower Back Leg B

1" dia. dowel for Rungs

3/4" dia.

3/4"

17 1/2"

7"

3/8" wide x 3/4" deep x 2" long mortise

7 1/2"

21"

16 1/2"

5 1/2"

Rung C

Front Leg A

7/8" dia.

16 1/2"

4"

10 1/2"

BACK LEG DETAIL

1 3/8"

1 1/8"

3"

1"

3/4"

7 1/2"

3 1/2"

1"

16 1/2"

7/8" dia.

1 1/2"

5 1/2"

Cutting List • Ladder-Back Chair

REF.	QTY.	PART	STOCK	THICK	WIDTH	LENGTH	COMMENTS
A	2	Front Legs	8/4 Cherry	1⅜ Dia.		18½	Add 1" to length for lathe work
B	2	Back Legs	Cherry	1⅜ Dia		42	Each back leg consists of two pieces
C	9	Rungs	Cherry	1 Dia.		15½	
D	3	Back Slats	4/4 Cherry	⅜	3½	15½	

Hardware

Tacks

1"-Wide Cloth Tape

Supplies

Carpenter's Glue

Water-Soluable Aniline Stain

Tung Oil

#600 Wet/Dry Paper

REQUIRED TOOLS

Lathe

Band saw

Drill

Sander (or sandpaper and block)

Spokeshave

Hammer

Turning the Rungs

All rungs (or stretchers), whether front, back or side, are identical and are turned in exactly the same manner. Mount the rung blanks between lathe centers and using a gouge, turn 1"-diameter spindles. On either end of these spindles turn a ¾"×⅞"-diameter stub. Make sure the ⅞" dimension is taken from the Forstner bit or drill bit that will be used to bore the mortises in the legs. This will ensure a snug fit between leg and rung. Bore a ⅞" hole in a scrap piece of wood and use this to test fit the rungs, or a template can be made, similar to the one shown in Tools and Techniques, to check this dimension without dismounting each spindle from the lathe. Sand each spindle while still on the lathe.

Turning the Front Legs

The front legs are made from 8⁄4 stock and the spindles are turned to 1⅝" cylinders. Before any turning is done, when the stock is still in a square condition, lay out and bore all holes. This will ensure correct placement of the holes and preclude trying to correctly bore holes on a turned cylinder, especially when holes have to be bored at 90° to each other.

Mount the front leg blanks between centers of the lathe, and using a roughing gouge, turn the blank to a 1⅝" cylinder. Measuring from the bottom of the leg, lay out the overall dimension of 18½". As can be seen, there is a remainder of stock that has to be cut off. This is accomplished by using a parting tool and cutting down to about a ¼" diameter at the 18½" dimension. Slightly round over the top and bottom edges of the leg using a parting and beading tool. Sand these legs while still on the lathe. Remove the completed leg from the lathe. The small piece of scrap must now be cut from the leg and the top portion of the leg sanded smooth.

Turning the Back Legs

Both of the back legs are made in two parts. The reason for this is the limitation of the distance between centers of my lathe (36" between centers). If you have a lathe that will accommodate greater than 42" between centers, the back legs can be made in one piece. Again, before any turning is done, bore all the rung holes. Additionally, cut all the slat mortises as indicated in the technical drawing. The 1" hole in the lower part, that joins the top and bottom portions of the back legs is bored after all turning has been completed.

Mount the blank on the lathe. The centering mark made by the drive center makes a convenient mark for boring the hole to join the top and bottom parts. With a roughing gouge, turn the bottom portions of both back legs to a dimension of 1⅝". Slightly round over both the top and bottom edges with a parting and beading tool. Scratch lines into the cylinders with a skew chisel. Not only will these marks disguise where the upper and lower portions are joined, but they will make the legs more attractive. Slightly round over these edges such that they will approximate the joining line between the top and lower portions. Sand these pieces and remove from the lathe. Bore a 1"-diameter hole, 1" deep into the top of the lower portion with a 1" Forstner bit.

The top portion of the back is turned to a 1⅝" diameter. Lay out the overall dimensions, and turn the top to a shape similar to the one shown in the technical drawing. There will be a stub of scrap material that must be removed from the top after all turning is completed. Turn a 1" stub on the bottom of this piece. Make sure that this dimension is the same as the 1" dimension found on the Forstner bit used to bore the hole in the lower portion, this will insure a snug fit between the top and bottom portions of the back legs. Slightly round over the stub end of the cylinder.

Making the Slats

The three slats are made from 4⁄4 stock, and instead of going through a complicated bending operation, the ⅜" thick slats can be resawed and shaped with a band saw. Referring to the technical drawing, trace this shape on each of the blanks and cut them out on a band saw, or if you don't have one, use a spokeshave to cut the shape. After the bend is shaped into the slats, cut the front view of the slat. Smooth these slats using a drum sander, and fit the slats to the mortises cut into the back legs.

Chair Assembly

Glue and clamp the three rungs to the front legs, and then glue and clamp the upper and lower portions of the back legs together. The three slats and two rungs are then glued and clamped to the back legs. Finally, all that remains to do is to glue and clamp the four side rungs to the front and rear assemblies.

Finishing

Before further work is done on the chair, the finish must be applied. For this project, I applied one coat of water- soluble aniline stain and four coats of tung oil. Between coats I sanded lightly with 600-grit wet/dry paper.

Seat

A number of seat types are possible for this chair, for example, real rush, fiber rush, splint or woven strips of colored cloth. For this project, I used two colors of woven cloth. This tape makes a beautiful-looking seat, wears well and is very easy to apply (see Weaving a Cloth Tape Chair Seat).

How to Even Lumber

1. Crosscut your board to about 1" longer than you want the finished board to be.

2. Now you'll cut a straight edge. Using a chalk line or a straight edge, mark a straight line about ½" wider than the final dimension down the length of the board. Then rip the lumber freehand with a band saw.

3. Next, surface one face of your board. Using push blocks, pass one face of the board over a jointer, making shallow cuts with each pass until the face is flat.

4. Place the new flat face against the jointer face and feed the ripped edge over the cutterhead so as to smooth out any flaws. Now you should have a right angle between the faced sides.

5. Now you'll plane the board. Place the flat side of the board face down in a planer and feed the board through. Plane down both sides of the board until you get the thickness you want. If you are going to finish sand later, remember to leave some extra material.

6. To cut your board to the finished width, use a table saw equipped with a rip fence. Place the jointed edge next to the rip fence and rip to the width you want, leaving an extra ¹⁄₁₆". Pass the board over the jointer to remove the excess material for a smoother surface.

7. For the last step, you'll cut your board to the finished length. Holding a miter gage firmly against the jointed edge of the board, pass the board through the blade enough to square off one end. Now turn the board around to the other end and cut to the final length. You may want to use a miter gage clamp for extra support if you're cutting large boards.

WEAVING A CLOTH TAPE CHAIR SEAT

A woven cloth chair seat is generally attributed to the Shakers and initially appeared in the early nineteenth century. The colors of tape available for such a project are numerous and offer many interesting design possibilities. Tapes come in 1" and ⅝" widths. Depending upon the tape used, a myriad of seat pattern designs are possible.

Definitions

Weavers have defined one length of tape wrapped around the seat rungs from front to back as a warp. The length of tape wrapped around the seat rungs from side to side is a woof. The woof is woven over and under the warp in the various patterns. In order to add a bit of comfort to the chair, and to prevent sagging of the tape, a 1" thickness of foam rubber is added between the upper and lower layers of the warp.

Tape comes in 5- and 10-yard rolls, (sometimes 20-yard rolls can be obtained). During the weaving of either the warp or the woof, it probably will be necessary to splice additional lengths of tape. A splice is made by overlapping two lengths of tape by about 1" and sewing them together with a few stitches. The splice should always be on the bottom side, where it's not visible.

Determining the Yardage

To determine the amount of tape needed for any project, follow these steps:

1. Measure the front rung between the posts in inches.
2. Measure the front to back distance in inches.
3. Multiply these two figures together.
4. Divide the resulting number by 9 to obtain the total number of yards for 1" tape (or divide by 5.3 for ⅝" tape).
5. If two different-colored tapes are to be used, order half the total number of yards per color.

The amount of 1" foam rubber that is necessary for any project is calculated by simply measuring the inside front-to-back and side-to-side dimensions. A small 1" triangle should be trimmed off the foam rubber on each of the four corners to keep any of the rubber

1 Tack the end of the tape to the inside rear edge of the side rung of the chair.

2 Continue wrapping until the front and back rungs cannot take any more tape. Then tack the end of the tape onto the rear of the front rung where the tacks will not be visible.

3 Insert the presized 1" thick foam rubber from one end, and carefully pull it through the warping.

from showing. If a two-color tape system is to be used, the darker color is traditionally wrapped from front to back (the warp).

Typical Supplies

- Cloth tape
- Foam rubber
- Needle and thread
- Hammer
- Upholstery tacks

Warping the Chair

Tack the end of the tape to the inside rear edge of the side rung of the chair, or, for a cleaner look, tack the tape onto the rear rung. Pull the tape up and over the back rung and forward to the front rung in a straight line

(see photo 1). Holding the tape tightly against the previous warp, pull the tape under the front rung to the back rung and over it. Continue this process until the front and back rungs cannot take any more tape. Tack the end of the tape on the rear of the front rung where the tacks will not be visible (see photo 2).

Stuffing the Warp

Insert the presized 1"-thick foam rubber from one end, and carefully pull it through the warping. Make sure the foam rubber is centered on the seat (see photo 3).

4 Tack the end of the tape at the rear end of one of the side rungs. Bring the tape up over the rung and start the weaving, going over and under the warp tapes in the particular pattern chosen.

5 After the weaving has been completed, take a look at the seat top, and make sure that the weave is straight.

6 Check that all the warps and woofs appear square. These can be straightened by either using your fingers or the back of a tea spoon.

Weaving the Woof

As was done with the warp, tack the end of the tape at the rear end of one of the side rungs. Bring the tape up over the rung and start the weaving, going over and under the warp tapes in the particular pattern chosen (see photo 4). Weave the underside of the seat in the same manner as the top. As the weaving continues, the seat will tighten up and the over and under weaving process will become more difficult. Use a flat-bladed screw-driver or the back of a tablespoon to push the tape end through the space between the warp and the foam rubber. When the last row is finished, either tack the end of the woof on the underside of the seat rung or sew it to a bottom warp.

Seats With Larger Front Rungs Than Back Rungs

Chairs with longer front rungs than back rungs have triangular spaces that have to be filled in with small pieces of warp. Spread the woof toward the rear of the side rung, and, tacking the end of the tape to the rung, weave the tape in the same pattern as the warp, first on the top, then on the bottom. Finally, tack the tape end to the rung. Reposition the tape previously spread. Follow this procedure until all blank spaces are filled.

Sofa Table

This small table is made of cherry and styled after Shaker furniture. It has clean, simple lines and offers two drawers and a platform for a lamp, candles and many other items.

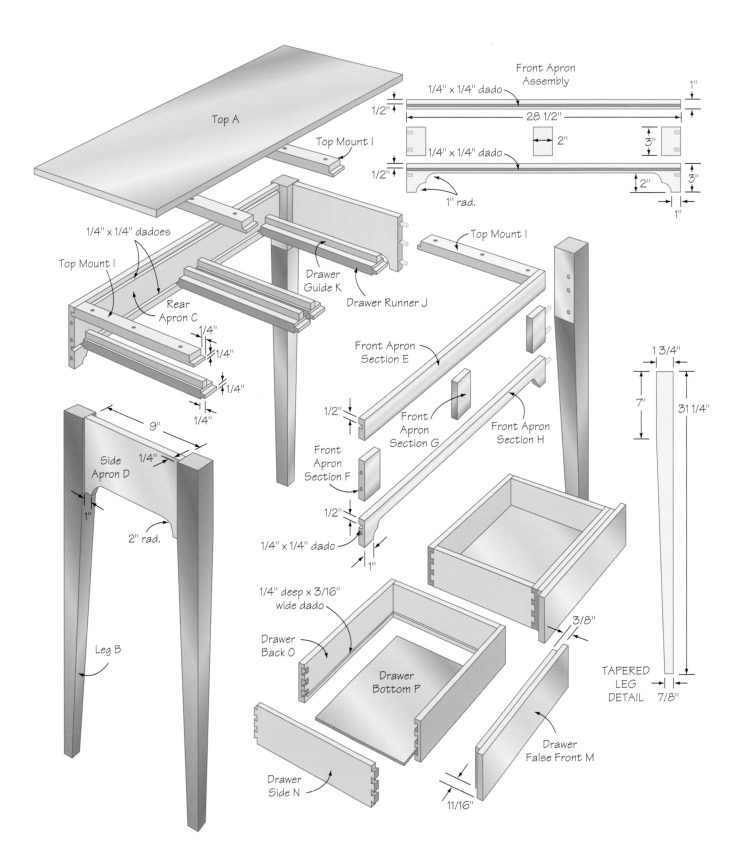

Top A

Front Apron Assembly

1/4" x 1/4" dado

28 1/2"

1"

1/2"

1/4" x 1/4" dado

2"

3"

1/2"

3"

2"

1" rad.

1"

Top Mount I

Top Mount I

1/4" x 1/4" dadoes

Top Mount I

Drawer Guide K

Rear Apron C

Drawer Runner J

Front Apron Section E

Top Mount I

1/4"

1/4"

1/4"

1/4"

1/2"

Front Apron Section G

Front Apron Section H

9"

1/4"

1 3/4"

Side Apron D

7"

31 1/4"

Front Apron Section F

1"

Leg B

2" rad.

1/2"

1/4" x 1/4" dado

1"

1/4" deep x 3/16" wide dado

3/8"

TAPERED LEG DETAIL

7/8"

Drawer Back O

Drawer Bottom P

Drawer False Front M

Drawer Side N

11/16"

Cutting List • Sofa Table

REF.	QTY.	PART	STOCK	THICK	WIDTH	LENGTH	COMMENTS
A	1	Top	4/4 Cherry	¾	14	36	
B	4	Legs	8/4 Cherry	¾	1¾	31¼	
C	1	Rear Apron	4/4 Cherry	¾	7	28½	
D	2	Side Aprons	4/4 Cherry	¾	7	9	
E	1	Front Rails	Cherry	¾	1	28½	
F	2	Front Ends	Cherry	¾	2	3	
G	1	Front Center	Cherry	¾	2	3	
H	1	Front Bottom Rail	Cherry	¾	3	28½	
I	4	Top Mounts	Poplar	¾	1½	11	
J	4	Drawer Runners	Poplar	¾	1½	11	
K	4	Drawer Guides	Cherry	½	½	10½	
L	4	Drawer Stops	Cherry	½	½	1	
M	2	Drawer False Fronts	Cherry	¾	3¾	12	
N	4	Drawer Sides	Poplar	½	2⅞	9¾	
O	4	Drawer Fronts & Backs	Poplar	½	2⅞	11 1/16	
P	2	Drawer Bottoms	Plywood	¼	9 11/16	10⅜	

Hardware

	2	1¼" Knobs
	24	⅜" Dia. x 1" Dowels
	12	#8 x 1¼" Wood Screws
	20	#6 x 1" Flathead Screws
	4	Drawer Tape (Rockler #70615)

Supplies

	Carpenter's Glue
	Tung Oil Varnish
	#600 Wet/Dry Paper
	Cabinet Wax
	0000 Steel Wool

REQUIRED TOOLS

Table or circular saw

Band saw

Tapering Jig

Jointer

Clamps

Sander

Planer

Router

Drill

Doweling Jig

Dovetail Jig

Making the Top

The top is made by jointing, gluing, and clamping enough ¼ stock to yield a 14"×36" surface. Smooth both sides by planing and sanding. Using a ¼" roundover router bit, round over all edges both top and bottom.

Making the Aprons

The rear apron is made from 4/4 stock. Lay out the shape shown in the technical drawing, but don't do any cutting yet. Set it aside until you have the front apron glued up.

The front apron is made by gluing and clamping five pieces of ¼ stock. Make sure the three 2"×3" center pieces have their grain running in the same horizontal direction to insure a correct appearance. As was done on the rear apron, lay out the shape as shown in the technical drawing, but don't cut it out yet.

On the rear of both the front and rear aprons, cut the ¼"×¼" dadoes. Using either a band saw or saber saw, cut the shapes on both aprons previously laid out. Sand both of these surfaces smooth with a drum sander. Round over this surface with a ¼" router roundover bit. The two side aprons are made from 7"×9" stock. Round over the bottom edge with a ¼" roundover router bit.

Making the Legs

The legs are made from 1¾"×1¾"×31¼" blanks (¾ stock). They are tapered on two sides. Tapering can be done using a simple jig as shown in Tools and Techniques. Adjust the tapering jig to approximately .44" at the 12" mark on the jig. With the tapering jig placed against the table saw fence, set the fence a distance of 1¾" inches from the 12" mark on the jig to the saw blade. Mark a 7½" line around each of the leg blanks. Place the leg blank against the taper stop and start the tapering cut at the 7½" mark by sliding the tapering jig toward the saw blade, continuing to the bottom of the leg. What results will be a taper on one side.

To taper the second side, just turn the leg blank 90° so that an untapered side is resting against the tapering jig. Cut the second taper, starting at the 7½" mark. Use this method to cut two sided tapers on all four legs.

Building the Mounts and Runners

Both the mounts and runners have the same dimensions and have their ends rabbeted as shown in the technical art. The sole difference between the mounts and runners is the oversized holes drilled into the mounts. These parts can be made from a secondary wood, such as poplar.

Assembly

Bore three ⅜"×½" holes in the ends of all apron pieces. Make sure the drill is perpendicular to the surface being bored. Use the doweling jig described in Tools and Techniques to determine where to bore the mating holes in the legs for the dowel pins. To use this jig, clamp the leg flat against the ¼" plywood. Place dowel centers in the ⅜" holes in the aprons. Hold the apron flat against the ¼" plywood, bottom side up, and press it firmly into the leg. What results will be three marks that can now be bored with a ⅜" bit to a depth of ½".

To keep everything in perspective, mark the mating legs and apron parts. The holes should only be bored on the tapered sides. Glue ⅜"×1" dowels into the aprons and glue and clamp the side aprons to their respective leg locations. After the glue has dried on the legs and side aprons, temporarily assemble the front and back aprons to the side assemblies and check for proper fit.

Mark the locations of the top mounts and drawer runners on the front and back aprons. Dry assemble the mounts and runners to the front and back aprons. Then dry assemble the front and back aprons to the leg subassembly with dowel pins. After proper fit, glue and clamp the assembly.

Building the Drawers

The drawers are constructed with dovetail joints, on both front and back. False drawer fronts are also added with knobs. Poplar is a good wood to use for the drawers. Although it is considered a secondary wood in furniture construction, it is a very easy wood to work with and finishes quite nicely. The false fronts are made from cherry and screwed to the drawer fronts with four #6×1" woodscrews.

Cut the drawer parts to their respective dimensions. Dovetails can either be cut by hand or be made using one of the many commercially available jigs. Cut a ¼"×¼" dado, ¼" up from the bottom of the fronts, backs and sides, to accept the plywood drawer bottoms. Using a ¼" router roundover bit, round over the top and bottom edges on the sides and backs. Glue and clamp the basic drawer.

Cut the drawer false fronts to the dimensions specified in the cutting list. Cut a ⅜"×⅜" rabbett on all back edges. Test fit both false fronts into their respective openings in the front apron to ensure a proper fit. Sand the drawer false fronts and screw them to the drawer fronts. Mount the drawer pull knobs.

Drawer Guides

Cut four ½"×½"×10½" drawer guides and drill three countersunk holes in each guide to accept three #6×1" flathead wood screws.

Slide the drawers in their respective slots and center them. Place the drawer guides, with the screws in the holes, next to the drawer sides and mark where the screws will be screwed on the drawer runners. Drill the pilot holes in the runners and screw down the guides. Test that the drawers slide in and out smoothly. As a finishing touch, add plastic glide strips, one on each drawer runner.

Tabletop Installation

With the top inverted on a bench, center the table carcase on the top. Insert the twelve #8×1¼" screws in the mounts and mark the pilot hole positions. Set your drill press up to drill the pilot holes, making sure not to drill completely through the top, a ½" depth max. Screw the top to the table carcase.

Finishing

I used a clear tung oil varnish as a finish for this project. Six coats were applied. The first two coats were wiped on with a rag. The following four coats were applied with lint-free Handiwipes, available at most auto supply stores. Each successive coat was applied after waiting at least 24 hours for the previous coats to dry. After the second coat, and after each ensuing coat, I sanded lightly with 600-grit wet/dry paper and wiped the project down with a tack rag. After about a week, I completed the finish with a cabinet wax applied with 0000 steel wool. I buffed the final finish with a clean soft rag.

Night Table

Placed beside a bed, this little table has a surface for a lamp, clock or radio, and offers a shelf for books and a drawer for sundry small items. Built from cherry, it will be a treasured possession for many years to come.

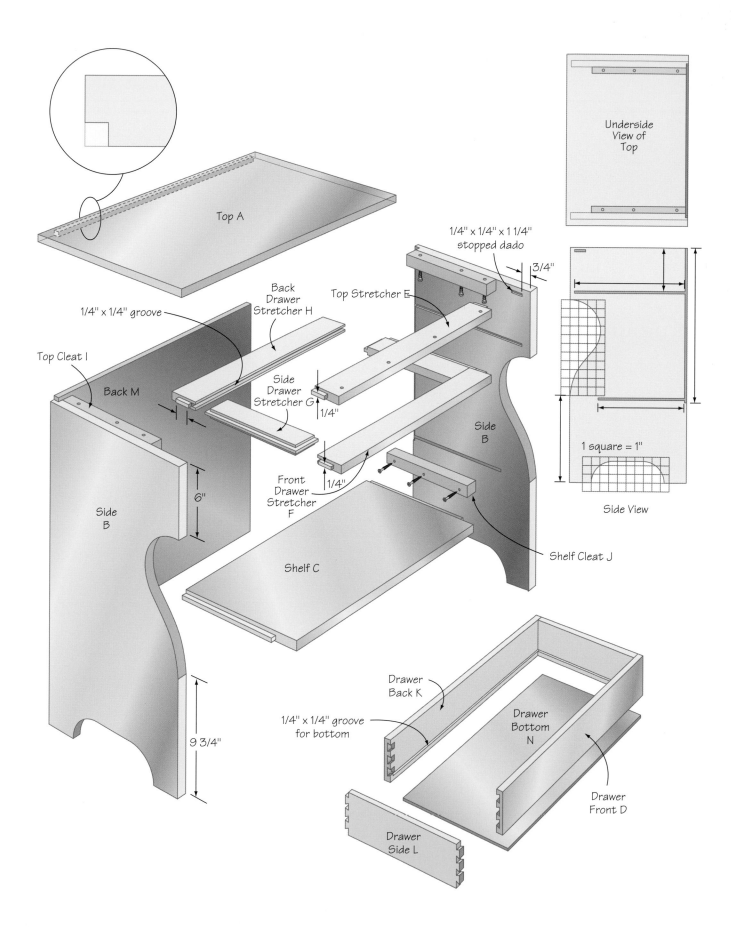

Top A

Underside View of Top

1/4" x 1/4" x 1 1/4" stopped dado

3/4"

Back Drawer Stretcher H

Top Stretcher E

1/4" x 1/4" groove

Top Cleat I

Back M

Side Drawer Stretcher G

1/4"

Side B

Side B

6"

Front Drawer Stretcher F

1/4"

Shelf Cleat J

Shelf C

1 square = 1"

Side View

9 3/4"

Drawer Back K

1/4" x 1/4" groove for bottom

Drawer Bottom N

Drawer Front D

Drawer Side L

Cutting List • Night Table

REF.	QTY.	PART	STOCK	THICK	WIDTH	LENGTH	COMMENTS
A	1	Top	Cherry	¾	14	20	
B	2	Sides	Cherry	¾	13½	27¼	
C	1	Shelf	Cherry	¾	11	17½	
D	1	Drawer Front	Cherry	¾	3^{13}⁄₁₆	16^{15}⁄₁₆	
E	1	Top Stretcher	Cherry	¾	1⅞	17½	
F	1	Bottom Stretcher	Cherry	¾	2	17½	
G	2	Side Stretchers	Cherry	¾	2	11¼	
H	1	Back Stretcher	Cherry	¾	2	17½	
I	2	Top Cleats	Cherry	¾	¾	10⅞	
J	2	Shelf Cleats	Cherry	¾	¾	8	
K	1	Drawer Back	Poplar	½	3^{13}⁄₁₆	16^{15}⁄₁₆	
L	2	Drawer Sides	Poplar	½	3^{13}⁄₁₆	11⅜	
M	1	Back	Plywood	¼	17^{7}⁄₁₆	17½	
N	1	Drawer Bottom	Cherry	¼	16^{7}⁄₁₆	11^{5}⁄₁₆	

Hardware

	1	¾" x ¾" x 2" Drawer Stop
	1	3" Bore Drawer Pull
	16	⅝" Brads
	32	#8 x 1¼" Wood Screws

Supplies

	Carpenter's Glue
	Gloss Polyurethane
	Satin Polyurethane
	#400 Wet/Dry Paper

REQUIRED TOOLS

Table saw

Band saw

Jointer

Clamps

Sander

Router

Drill

Dovetail Jig

Building the Top

The top is made by edge jointing, and gluing up enough stock to yield a 14"×20" blank. Rout a ¼"×¼"×18" inch stopped rabbet in the bottom rear edge of the top to accommodate a portion of the back panel. Using a ½" roundover router bit, round over both the top edges of the sides and front, and then sand the top smooth.

Making the Sides

Glue up and size two panels 13½"×27". Trace the outline as shown in the technical drawing. Before cutting these curves, do all other operations on the side panels.

Rout the stopped dadoes (there are three on each panel) and the stopped rabbets. With these operations complete, the curves can be cut and smoothed.

Round over and blend the edges of these curves into the straight edges. Use a ⅜" roundover bit to do this operation. Sand the side panels smooth.

Making the Shelf

Glue up and size stock for the shelf to the overall size of 11"×17½". Cut ¼" tenons on either end of the shelf. Size each tenon to 9⅝". These tenons should fit comfortably into the stopped dadoes previously routed into the sides. Round over both front edges with a ⅜" roundover bit. Sand the shelf smooth.

Making the Stretchers

Cut all stretchers to size. Note that the top stretcher has two ¼" stub tenons on either end that have to be sized to fit the 1¼" stopped dado. Drill four oversized holes to accommodate #8×1¼" wood screws. The oversized holes are to allow for seasonal shrinking and swelling of wood. The front and back drawer stretchers have a ¼" dado cut into them in order to accept the tenons from the side drawer stretchers. Additionally, the ends each have a ¼" stub tenon sized to fit the stopped dado slots in the side.

Cut a ¼" tongue on each of the side drawer stretchers, as well as ¼" tenons sized to fit the front and back drawer stretchers.

Making the Back

Make the back from a piece of ¼" hardwood plywood cut to 17⁷⁄₁₆"×17½".

Cabinet Assembly

Dry assemble the cabinet and determine the exact locations of the side stretchers and the cleats. Glue the stretchers to the sides. Screw the shelf cleats in place with #8×1¼" wood screws. The top cleats are screwed to the top with #8×1¼" wood screws. Don't glue the cleats to the top. This will allow for the seasonal movement of wood. Glue and screw one side of the shelf to the side. Screw the top to the sides using the two top cleats. Finally, assemble the remaining side and stretchers. Glue and nail the back to the assembly with ⅝" brads.

Making the Drawers

The drawers are constructed with dovetail joints, on both front and back. These joints add strength to the drawer and a little bit of class to the project. The dovetails can be cut using one of the many commercially available router jigs, or, if you feel adventurous, you can cut the pins and tails by hand. Either way it is done, the dovetail is an elegant joint. Mount the drawer pull.

Drawer Stop

After the drawer has been asssmbled, measure the front-to-back dimension and transfer this measurement to the top surface of the back drawer stretcher. Glue and clamp the ¾"×¾"×2" drawer stop here.

Finishing

The finish for a project such as this is really a matter of personal preference. Since this piece was constructed from cherry wood, I decided not to stain the wood and allowed the wood to assume its own natural, warm patina over a period of time. I applied one coat of gloss polyurethane, followed by two coats of satin polyurethane. Between coats I sanded lightly with 400-grit wet/dry paper and wiped down after each sanding with a tack rag.

Common Wood Defects

KNOT A dark whorl from a cross section of a branch. Knots weaken wood and affect appearance.

BARK POCKETS Encased area of bark in board. Bark pockets reduce strength and lessen appearance.

INSECT DAMAGE Insects can cause holes in boards that reduce board strength.

FUNGAL DAMAGE Fungi can stain wood. Called spalting, wood with advanced fungal decay may be weakened, and when cut, will release spores that can cause severe allergic reactions.

CHECK A separation between growth rings at the end of a board. Checks are common and lessen appearance, but do not weaken wood unless deep.

SHAKE A separation between growth rings that results in a slat coming loose from the face of the board.

GUM A sticky accumulation of resin that bleeds through finishes.

PITCH POCKETS Pitch-filled spaces between grain layers. May bleed after board is milled; occasionally bleeds through finishes.

MACHINE BURN Blunt planer knives may burn the face of the board.

MACHINE WAVES Incorrect planer speeds may create waves on the face of the wood. Boards with waves must be thinned again.

BOW An end-to-end warp along the face of the board. Bowed boards are fit for horizontal load-bearing if placed convex side up.

CUP An edge-to-edge warp across the face of the board. Cupped boards are fit for nonload-bearing use if placed convex side up or out.

CROOK An end-to-end warp along the board edge. Fit for horizontal load-bearing if placed convex side up.

TWIST A lop-sided or uneven warp. Wood is weakened, but twisted boards are fit for nonload-bearing use.

Lamp Table

This quaint little table will be at home lighting a portion of a large room or filling a small spot in an entrance way. Built of cherry and finished with a clear tung oil varnish, it can only add to the beauty of a home.

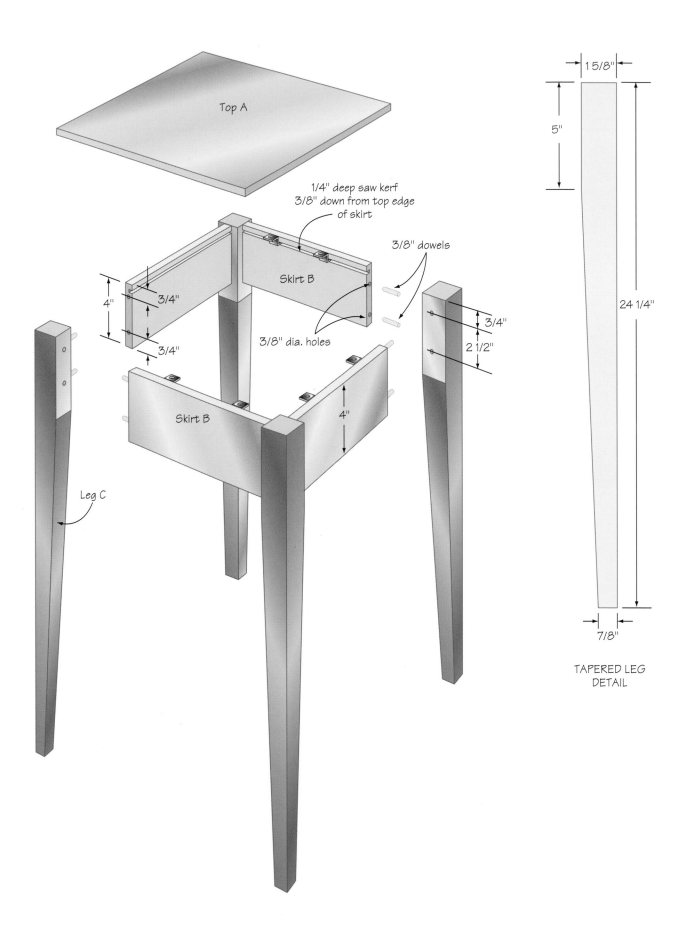

Top A

1/4" deep saw kerf
3/8" down from top edge
of skirt

3/8" dowels

Skirt B

4"

3/4"

3/4"

3/8" dia. holes

Skirt B

4"

3/4"

2 1/2"

Leg C

1 5/8"

5"

24 1/4"

7/8"

TAPERED LEG
DETAIL

Cutting List • Lamp Table

REF.	QTY.	PART	STOCK	THICK	WIDTH	LENGTH	COMMENTS
A	1	Top	Cherry	¾	16	16	
B	4	Sides	Cherry	¾	8¾	4	
C	4	Legs	8/4 Cherry	1⅝	1⅝	24¼	

Hardware

16	⅜" Dia. x 1" Dowels	
8	Fasteners (Woodcraft #27N10)	

Supplies

- Carpenter's Glue
- Clear Tung Oil Varnish
- #600 Wet/Dry Paper
- Cabinet Wax
- 0000 Steel Wool

Required Tools

- Table saw
- Band saw
- Jointer
- Clamps
- Sander
- Router
- Drill
- Dovetail Jig
- Tapering jig
- Doweling jig

Making the Top

Joint, glue and clamp enough stock to make up a 16"×16"×¾" blank. When the glue has dried, size the blank to the dimensions listed in the bill of materials. Sand the blank and round over all edges with a ¼" roundover router bit.

Making the Sides

Cut out the four sides to the dimensions listed in the bill of materials. Run a saw-kerf along the top inside portion of each of the four sides, about ¼" deep. Lay out and bore two ⅜" holes, ⅝" deep, in the ends of each side blank. Round over the lower, outer edge of each side.

Making the Legs

The leg blanks can be made from ¾ material, or they can be glued up from ¼ stock. Whichever method is used, size these blanks to a length of 24¼". As can be seen in the technical drawing, the legs are tapered. This is a simple operation if a jig such as is shown in Tools and Techniques is used in conjunction with a table saw. Even the mathematics for this method is simple. The resultant taper calculation number can be set on the taper jig at the 12" point with a vernier caliper (e.g., Stanley 35-019).

Mark a 5" line around each of the leg blanks. The tapering jig is placed against the table saw fence. Set the saw blade's distance following the instructions given in the tools and techniques section. Place a leg blank against the jig and slide the jig toward the saw blade, continuing until a taper is cut. To taper the second side, rotate the blank 90° and cut the second taper starting at the 5" mark on the leg blank. Continue this process until all four blanks are tapered.

Doweling the Legs and Sides

In order to carry out the following operations, it is necessary to have ⅜" dowel centers. Build a dowel-locating jig similar to that shown in Tools and Techniques. Clamp the leg to the jig. Place the ⅜" centers into the ⅜" holes previously bored in the sides. Tap the side into the leg blank. Two locating marks on the leg blank will result. Bore a ⅜" hole with a Forstner bit at each locating mark to a depth of ⅝". This procedure is followed for all side-leg connections. Note that holes should only be bored on the tapered sides. Cut sixteen ⅜"×1" dowels. Select two legs and a side and temporarily dry assemble them to the side with the dowels. The legs should fit snugly and be square with the side. Glue and clamp these parts together. Continue this operation with another set of two legs and a side. When the glue is dried on both these subassemblies, glue and clamp the remaining two sides to the two subassemblies.

Assembly of the Top to the Leg Subassembly

The top is connected to the leg subassembly by means of eight tabletop fasteners. The use of these little pieces of hardware will allow the top wood to seasonally shrink and swell without the wood splitting. Invert the top on the bench, and center the leg subassembly on the top. Insert the table fasteners into the saw-kerf in the sides (two fasteners per side). Mark the location of the screw holes for the fasteners. Drill pilot holes (make sure not to drill completely through the top), and screw the fasteners to the top.

Finishing

Apply three coats of clear tung oil varnish. Sand lightly between coats with 600-grit wet/dry paper. After each sanding, wipe the project down with a tack rag in order to remove all sanding particles. Finally, apply a coat of cabinet wax and buff.

Wood Color Guide

COLOR	WOOD	COST	NOTES
White	Aspen	$	
	Silver Maple	$$	
	Spruce (adirondack spruce, blue spruce, skunk spruce)	$	
	Eastern white pine	$	Pines have high pitch content that can ruin blades—use blade lubricant
	Sugar pine	$$	See above
	Western white pine	$	See above
	Holly	$$$	Discolors if the wood is not cut properly
	Basswood (American lime)	$	Turns pale brown on exposure
	Hard maple (rock maple, sugar maple)	$$	
	European ash (English/French/etc. ash)	$$	Turns light brown on exposure
Black	Black walnut	$$	
	Wenge	$$$	
	South American walnut	$$$	
	Ebony (gaboon)	$$$	Difficult to machine; endangered
Red	Bloodwood (Brazil red wood, cardinal wood, pau rainha)	$$$	Cuts poorly—use #9 Precision Ground blade on band saw
	Aromatic cedar (eastern red cedar, chest cedar, Tennessee cedar)	$	Often has internal stress cracks—when cutting into small pieces, wood may break
	Cherry	$$	
	Jarrah	$$	Moderately difficult to work
	Brazilwood (pernambuco wood, bahia wood, parn wood)	$$$	Endangered
	African padauk (camwood, barwood)	$$	Endangered
	Red heart	$$$	
Yellow	Pau amarillo	$$	Brightest—canary yellow
	Orange osage	$$	Turns orange-brown on exposure
	Yellow cedar (Alaska cedar, nootka-cypress, yellow-cypress)	$$	
	Yellow pine	$	
	Ponderosa pine (western yellow pine, Californian white pine)	$	Knots can cause problems when planing
	Caragana	$	Actually a shrub—have to look for it
	Hickory	$$	
	Yellowheart	$$	
	Satinwood (East Indian satinwood)	$$$	Moderately difficult to work
	Obeche (ayous, wawa, arere)	$	Keep cutting edges sharp; endangered
Green	Staghorn sumac (velvet sumac)	$	Grows as shrub/small tree—not commercially available—grows in NE U.S. and eastern Canada
	American yellow poplar (tuliptree, canary wood, canoe wood)	$	Must search out green or gray heartwood
	Vera wood (maracaibo, lignum-vitae, guyacan)	$$$	Hard to cut; hard to get finish to stick because wood is oily/waxy; durathane finish will highlight color; finish pieces before gluing project
Blue/Gray	Spruce (Adirondack spruce, blue spruce, skunk spruce)	$	Some spruce boards have gray or blue cast-rare
	Blue mahoe (mahoe, mountain mahoe, seasise mahoe)	$$$	Heartwood varies from purple, metallic blue, olive brown—must search for blue—rare
Purple	Purple heart (violet wood, pauroxo, coracy)	$$	Burns easily—use Precision Ground scroll saw blade or band saw; be careful not to burn wood while sanding
Orange	Orange osage	$$	Cuts yellow, then turns orange on exposure
	African padauk (comwood, barwood, corail)	$$	Heartwood can be found in bright orange hue
	Zebra wood	$$$	Dark streaks through wood
	Red gum (sweetgum, alligator wood, hazel pine)	$$	Streaks of red and black; beautiful grain

Legend:
    $ Free or inexpensive
    $$ Moderately priced
    $$$ Expensive

Small Drawer Table

This table features the Shaker look along with tapered legs and a white porcelain pull. Made of cherry and given a polyurethane finish, this elegant piece will be at home in any room of the house.

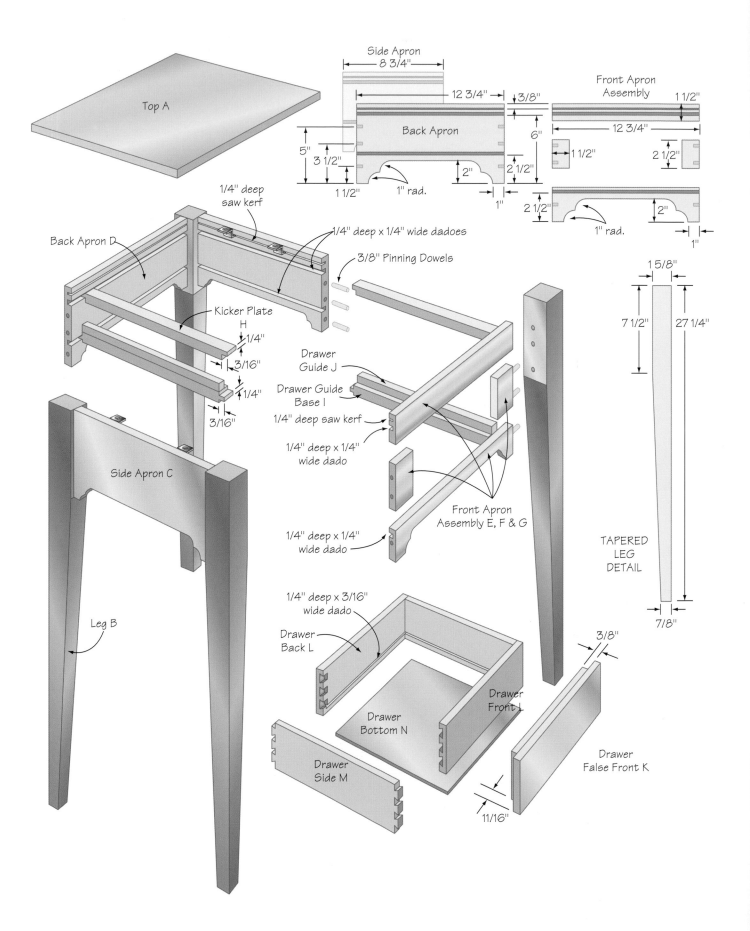

Top A

Side Apron
8 3/4"

Back Apron

12 3/4"

3/8"

6"

5"

3 1/2"

2"

2 1/2"

1 1/2"

1" rad.

1"

Front Apron
Assembly

1 1/2"

12 3/4"

1 1/2"

2 1/2"

2 1/2"

2"

1" rad.

1"

1/4" deep
saw kerf

Back Apron D

1/4" deep x 1/4" wide dadoes

3/8" Pinning Dowels

Kicker Plate
H

1/4"

3/16"

1/4"

3/16"

Drawer
Guide J

Drawer Guide
Base I

1/4" deep saw kerf

1/4" deep x 1/4"
wide dado

Front Apron
Assembly E, F & G

1/4" deep x 1/4"
wide dado

1 5/8"

7 1/2"

27 1/4"

7/8"

TAPERED
LEG
DETAIL

Side Apron C

Leg B

1/4" deep x 3/16"
wide dado

Drawer
Back L

Drawer
Bottom N

Drawer
Front J

Drawer
Side M

Drawer
False Front K

3/8"

11/16"

Cutting List • Small Drawer Table

REF.	QTY.	PART	STOCK	THICK	WIDTH	LENGTH	COMMENTS
A	1	Top	4/4 Cherry	3/4	16	24	
B	4	Legs	8/4 Cherry	1 5/8	1 5/8	27 1/4	
C	2	Side Aprons	Cherry	3/4	7	8 3/4	
D	1	Back Apron	Cherry	3/4	7	12 3/4	
E	1	Upper Front Apron	Cherry	3/4	1 1/2	12 3/4	
F	1	Lower Front Apron	Cherry	3/4	3	12 3/4	
G	2	Side Front Aprons	Cherry	3/4	1 1/2	2 1/2	
H	2	Kicker Plates	Cherry	3/4	1 1/4	10 5/16	
I	2	Drawer Guide Bases	4/4 Poplar	3/4	1 1/4	10 5/16	
J	2	Drawer Guides	4/4 Poplar	3/4	3/4	9 5/16	
K	1	False Front	Cherry	3/4	3 1/2	11	
L	2	Drawer Front & Back	Poplar	1/2	2 3/8	9 5/8	
M	2	Drawer Sides	Poplar	1/2	2 3/8	9	
N	1	Drawer Bottom	Plywood	1/4	9	9 1/8	

Hardware

	6	#6 x 1" Wood Screws
	1	1 1/4"-Dia. Knob
	12	Fasteners (Woodcraft #27N10)
	24	3/8" x 1 1/2" Dowels

Supplies

	Carpenter's Glue
	Drawer Tape (Rockler #70615)
	Clear Semigloss Waterborne Acrylic Polyurethane
	#600 Wet/Dry Paper
	Cabinet Wax

Required Tools

- Jointer
- Clamps
- Plane
- Router
- Table saw
- Band saw or saber saw
- Drill
- Dovetail jig
- Tapering jig
- Doweling jig
- Dowel centers
- Sander (or sandpaper and block)

Building the Top

The top is made by edge jointing, gluing and clamping enough ¼ stock to yield a 16"×24" surface. After the glue has dried, smooth both sides by planing and sanding. Using a ¼" roundover router bit, round over all edges, both top and bottom.

Making the Legs

The legs are made from 8/4 stock and sized to the 1⅝" dimension, or they can also be glued up from 4/4 stock. Whichever method is used, cut all four to an overall length of 27¼". The leg blanks are then tapered on two sides. The tapering operation can be done using a jig as shown in Tools and Techniques. The tapering operation is started at a dimension of 7½" from the top of each leg blank. After one side is tapered, turn the blank 90° and taper the second side.

Building the Side and Back Aprons

Cut the back apron and the two side aprons to the dimensions listed in the bill of materials. Trace scallops on the bottom of each apron blank. Cut out the shape of the scallops with either a coping saw or a band saw. Smooth the curves using files and sand paper or on a spindle sander if you have one.

Building the Front Apron Assembly

Cut all the parts as listed in the bill of materials. Glue and clamp the side pieces to the rest of the assembly. After the glue has dried, sand the front surfaces smooth. Trace the shape of the scallops on the bottom of the assembly, cut them out and sand the curves smooth. Cut a ¼"-deep saw-kerf on the top rear of all four aprons. These kerfs will serve to attach the top to the table. Cut ¼" dadoes on the rear of both the front and rear aprons as shown in the technical drawing. Using a ¼" roundover bit, round over the lower edge of all aprons.

Joining the Aprons to the Legs

These parts are joined using ⅜" dowels and a simple doweling jig such as is described in the section on tools and techniques. Bore ⅜" holes in the apron ends as shown in the technical drawing to a depth of ¾". Cut twenty-four ⅜" dowels 1½" in length. If using the jig described in Tools and Techniques, clamp the top of the leg against the end of the ¼" plywood. Insert ⅜" dowel centers in the ⅜" holes bored in the aprons. Hold the apron flat against the ¼" plywood, bottom side up. Press firmly into the leg. What results are three marks that can now be bored with a ⅜" bit to a depth of ¾". Mark the mating legs and apron parts. The holes should only be bored on the tapered sides.

Glue the ⅜"×1½" dowels into the side aprons. Glue and clamp the side aprons to their respective locations. After the glue has dried, temporarily assemble the front and back aprons to the side assemblies and check for proper fit. Then glue and clamp the side assemblies to the front and back aprons.

Drawer Construction

Cut out the false front to the dimensions in the bill of materials. Make a ⅜"×¹¹⁄₁₆" rabbet on the inside ends and a ⅜"×⁹⁄₁₆" rabbet on the inside top and bottom. Sand the false front and round over the front edge with a ¼" roundover router bit.

The drawer assembly is made from ¼ poplar sized to a thickness of ½". This project as described has dovetail joints joining the drawer assembly. These joints were made using a dovetail jig. As you are aware, there are many such jigs on the market, any of which will suffice. Dovetail joints can also be cut individually by hand. Whichever method is used, cut the joints so that a tight fit results. Cut ¼"-deep dadoes along the bottom inside edge of each of the drawer parts, L and M. The drawer bottom will fit in this slot. Cut the drawer bottom to the dimensions shown in the bill of materials. Dry assemble the drawer to see that all parts fit. Sand all parts and glue the drawer together. Screw the drawer false front to the drawer assembly.

Kicker Plates and Drawer Guides

Cut out and size all the parts to the dimensions shown in the bill of materials. Rabbet the ends of H and J. Part I is glued and screwed to J as shown in the technical drawing.

Insert and glue the kicker plates in the dadoes of the front and back aprons, as shown in the technical drawing. Insert the drawer guide assemblies in the dadoes, but do not glue them in place. The drawer assembly is now used as a gauge to set the drawer guide positions and assure proper gliding of the drawer. When the correct position of each drawer guide is determined, glue them in place. In order to help the drawer slide in and out more smoothly, cut two 10" pieces of drawer tape and stick it on each of the drawer guide bases.

Assembly of Top to Leg Subassembly

The top is connected to the leg subassembly by means of twelve tabletop fasteners. The use of these little pieces of hardware will allow the top to seasonally shrink and swell without the wood splitting. Invert the top on the bench. Center the leg subassembly on the top. Insert the table fasteners into the saw-kerfs in the sides (three fasteners per side). Mark the location of the screw holes for the fasteners. Drill pilot holes (make sure you don't drill completely through the top) and screw the fasteners to the top.

Finishing

Since I used cherry, no stain was applied. The wood was allowed to naturally darken to its own beautiful color. I applied three coats of a clear semigloss waterborne acrylic polyurethane and lightly sanded between coats with 600-grit wet/dry paper. After each sanding, I wiped the project down with a tack rag to remove the sanding dust. After the finish had dried, I applied a coat of cabinet wax and buffed the entire table.

Common Sizes of Shelf-Storage Objects

When building bookcases, entertainment units, or any piece of furniture that is meant to hold things, use these handy dimensions to figure out the needed space for these common items:

	OBJECT	DEPTH × HEIGHT (INCHES)
Books	Paperback	$4\frac{1}{4} \times 6\frac{7}{8}$
	Standard Hardback	$7 \times 9\frac{1}{2}$
	Large Book (i.e. Textbook)	9×11
	Art/Coffee Table Book	11×15
Music	Vinyl LP	$12\frac{3}{8} \times 12\frac{3}{8}$
	Compact Disc	$5\frac{1}{2} \times 5$
	Audiocassette	$2\frac{3}{4} \times 4\frac{1}{4}$
Video	Laser Disc	$12\frac{3}{8} \times 12\frac{3}{8}$
	DVD	$12\frac{3}{8} \times 12\frac{3}{8}$
	VHS Videocassette	$4\frac{1}{8} \times 7\frac{1}{2}$
	8mm VHS	$4\frac{1}{8} \times 7\frac{1}{2}$
Computer	CD-ROM	$5\frac{1}{2} \times 5$
	$3\frac{1}{2}$" Floppy Disc	$3\frac{1}{2} \times 3\frac{1}{2}$
	$5\frac{1}{4}$" Floppy Disc	$5\frac{1}{4} \times 5\frac{1}{4}$

Wall Sconces

Here is a delightful wall sconce that can be made to hold either one or two candles, whichever you prefer. This is accomplished by varying the horizontal plate and turning two candle cups and two finials on your lathe.

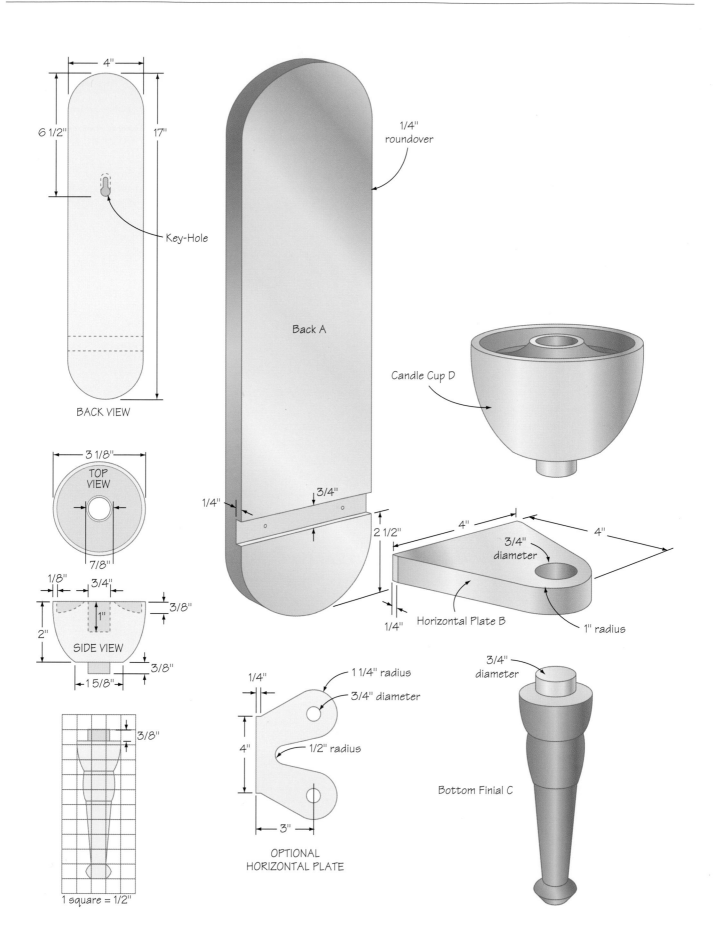

4"

6 1/2"   17"

Key-Hole

BACK VIEW

1/4"
roundover

Back A

Candle Cup D

3 1/8"

TOP
VIEW

7/8"

1/8"   3/4"   3/8"

2"   1"   SIDE VIEW

1 5/8"   3/8"

3/8"

1 square = 1/2"

1/4"   3/4"

2 1/2"

1/4"

4"   4"

3/4"
diameter

Horizontal Plate B   1" radius

1/4"   1 1/4" radius

3/4" diameter

4"   1/2" radius

3"

OPTIONAL
HORIZONTAL PLATE

3/4"
diameter

Bottom Finial C

Cutting List • Wall Sconces

REF.	QTY.	PART	STOCK	THICK	WIDTH	LENGTH	COMMENTS
A	1	Back	Oak	¾	4	17	
B	1	Horizontal Plate	Oak	¾	4	4	For two candles, increase to ¾ x 4¼ x 6½
C	1	Bottom Finial	Oak	1½ Dia.		6	Make two of these for two-candle sconce
D	1	Candle Cup	Oak	3⅛ Dia.		4	Make two of these for two-candle sconce

Hardware

	2	#6 x 1" Flathead Wood Screws
	1 (or 2)	2⅝" x 10" Glass Chimney
	1 (or 2)	⅞"-Dia. Candlestick Eyelet (Constantine's #99U8)

Supplies

	Carpenter's Glue
	Golden Oak Stain
	Gloss Polyurethane
	Satin Polyurethane
	#600 Wet/Dry Paper

REQUIRED TOOLS

Table or circular saw

Dado set

Lathe

Router

Drill or drill press

Spindle sizing jig

Sander (or sandpaper and block)

Making the Back

Cut the back to size on the table saw and using a dado set, plough a ¾"×¼" deep dado. Reverse the back blank and lay out the dimension for the wall-mounting keyhole. With a router keyhole bit, attached to either a router or a drill press, cut a slot as shown in the technical drawing. Lay out and cut a 2" radius on each end of the blank. Sand the curves smooth. Using a router, round over the front edge of the back with a ¼" roundover bit. Drill two holes in the dado center to accommodate two #6×1" flathead wood screws. Countersink these two holes on the rear side of the back.

Horizontal Plate

Decide whether you want a single- or double-candle horizontal plate, and refer to the technical drawing for the dimensions for both. Lay out the horizontal plate appropriately, depending on your choice, on a piece of ¾" stock. Cut out the plate to the overall dimensions. Bore the ¾" hole(s) using a ¾" Forstner bit. Sand the edges smooth and round over both top and bottom edges with a ¼" roundover router bit.

Assembly of Horizontal Plate to the Back

Fit the plate into the back, insert the two screws into the back and spot the screw holes in the rear of the plate. Drill two pilot holes into the plate to accommodate the two #6×1" wood screws. Glue and screw the plate to the back.

Turning the Bottom Finial

Mount the 1½"×6" blank between centers on the lathe. Using a roughing gouge, turn the blank to a cylinder. Lay out the length dimensions on the blank. Start at the tail stock of the lathe and, with a pencil, mark the dimensions of ⅜", 1⅜", 2⅜", 4½" and 5". You will notice that there is a remainder of wood of about an inch at the head stock end of the lathe. This is scrap and will be cut off and discarded at the end of the turning process. With a parting tool, starting at the tail stock, cut down to the diameters of ¾", 1", ⅞", ½" and ⅞" at your pencil marks. Clear out the rest of the ¾" dimension, and ensure that it will fit snugly in the hole bored in the horizontal plate. Use a sizing fixture similar to the one shown in Tools and Techniques.

With a spindle gouge, turn the first three shapes as shown in the technical drawing. Again using a parting tool, and referring to the bottom end of the finial (just below the ½" mark), cut a groove to a depth of about ⅝". This is necessary in order to be able to shape the bottom of the finial.

With a parting and beading tool, round over and shape the bottom of the finial to a shape similar to that shown. The shape can be varied, the limits being the ¾" dimension and your imagination. Sand the completed finial while it is still between centers. Take the finial off the lathe and cut off the scrap piece attached. Sand the bottom edge smooth. Glue the finial into the bottom of the horizontal plate.

Installing the Candle Cup

The turning blank for a candle cup is made from either a solid chunk of stock or stock that is glued up from thinner wood. Whichever method is used, the result should be a blank measuring 3⅛×3⅛×4". The added length of about 1⅝" will be used to hold the turning between centers of the lathe and will be cut off later.

Place the sized turning blank between centers of the lathe, and with a roughing gouge, turn the blank to a 3⅛" cylinder. Starting from the tail stock end of the lathe, mark the 2" and ⅜" dimensions. With the parting tool cut the ⅜" dimension, leaving a ¾" stub. Make sure that this dimension makes a snug fit with the ¾" hole bored in the horizontal plate. Mark the 1⅝" dimension on the stub end of the blank as shown in the technical drawing.

Using a gouge, shape the side of the blank to a form similar to that in the drawing. Mark the ⅛" and 1" dimensions on the end of the blank, and with a parting tool, turn a slot ⅜" deep. Using a gouge, slope the surface. Sand the entire candle cup and remove from the lathe.

Cut the scrap end piece from the cup and make a test fit with the horizontal plate. Using a ⅞" Forstner bit, bore a hole 1" deep into the top of the cup. Press the candlestick eyelet into the hole. When doing this operation, insert it with uniform pressure. This can be accomplished by using the drill press as an arbor press to exert this pressure. Glue the candle cup into the plate.

Finishing

Depending upon the species of wood used for this project, the finishing will vary; however, for the project I have described, I used oak and applied one coat of golden oak stain. I followed this with one coat of gloss polyurethane and two coats of satin polyurethane. Between coats, I sanded lightly with 600-grit wet/dry paper and wiped down the project after each sanding with a tack rag. Finally, mount the sconce on the wall, put in candles of your choice, install the glass chimney and enjoy.

Shop Wisdom

- Make sure you have a pushstick or pushblock within easy reach before starting a cut or machining operation. Don't get into awkward positions where a sudden slip could make your hand hit the blade or cutter.

- Double-check your wood for loose knots, nails, and other hazards. If not noticed, these can cause injury and damage your equipment.

- Always wear goggles, safety glasses, or a face mask when using cutting tools. When sanding, wear a dust mask as well. If you're using an extremely loud tool, wear hearing protection. Never wear neckties, work gloves, bracelets/wristwatches, or loose clothing. For long hair, wear a cap or tie it back.

- Be sure your guards and anti-kickback devices are in good working order and in their correct positions. Before using a blade or cutter, check to make sure it is sharp and clean.

- For your workshop, make sure the floor surface is hard wearing, non trip-and-slip (no steps, level changes, slopes), fireproof, easy to clean, and dry. Most woodworkers have a solid concrete slab. For additional traction (for instance, in front of a lathe), a low-cost solution is to paint a selected area of floor with rubber-type adhesive, sprinkle sand on it, and sweep away the remaining sand after the adhesive has dried. Additionally, rubber mats serve as portable non-slip and anti-fatigue floor surfaces.

- Some specific tasks (or left- and right-handedness) can require additional or adjustable lighting. You may want to install lamps as side lights where more light is needed. Portable light stands are also helpful.

- Provide visitors, especially children, with safety goggles and make sure they're a safe distance away. Keep in mind that many machines (for instance, portable planers) spit out waste at child's-eye level. If you have a workshop at home with children, educate them in the safe use of the machines. When not in the workshop, remove start-up keys and lock the workshop. You may want to consider padlocking the machines.

- Every woodshop needs fire detection and prevention equipment. Install smoke or fire detectors, and keep at least one class ABC fire extinguisher in an easy access location. Never throw water onto live machinery.

Dressing Mirror

Whether hanging over a dressing table or just on the wall, this attractive mirror is a welcome addition to any bedroom setting. This project is made from 5/4 cherry and features mortise and tenon joints on all four corners, which assures strong construction.

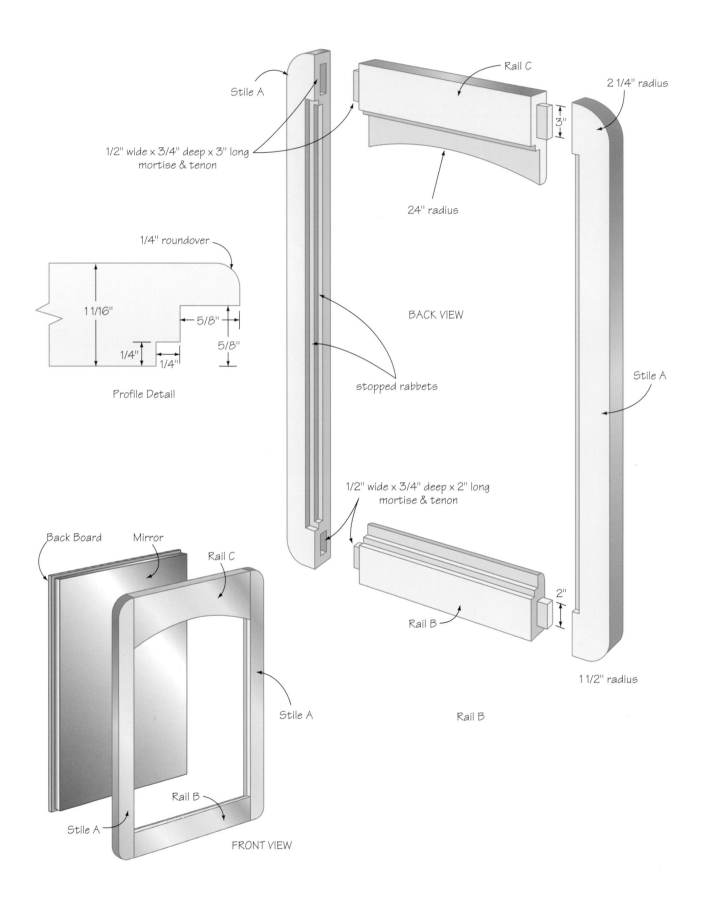

Stile A

1/2" wide x 3/4" deep x 3" long
mortise & tenon

Rail C

2 1/4" radius

3"

24" radius

1/4" roundover

1 1/16"

5/8"

1/4"

1/4"

5/8"

Profile Detail

BACK VIEW

Stile A

stopped rabbets

1/2" wide x 3/4" deep x 2" long
mortise & tenon

Back Board

Mirror

Rail C

2"

Rail B

Stile A

1 1/2" radius

Stile A

Rail B

Rail B

Stile A

FRONT VIEW

Cutting List • Dressing Mirror

REF.	QTY.	PART	STOCK	THICK	WIDTH	LENGTH	COMMENTS
A	2	Stiles	5/4 Cherry	1 1/16	2 1/2	36	
B	1	Bottom Rail	5/4 Cherry	1 1/16	3 1/2	20 1/2	
C	1	Top Rail	5/4 Cherry	1 1/16	7	20 1/2	
	1	Back	Hardboard	1/4	19 11/16	29 1/8	Measure after frame is assembled
	1	Foam Board	Foamboard	1/8	19 11/16	28 1/2	Measure after frame is assembled

Hardware

	20	#4 x 3/4" Flathead Wood Screws
	2	Mirror Hangers (Woodcraft #27K02)
		1/8" Copper Wire

Supplies

		Carpenter's Glue
		Gloss Polyurethane
		Satin Polyurethane
		#400 Wet/Dry Paper

Stiles and Rail Operations

Three operations have to be performed on the two stiles:

1. routing stopped rabbets
2. mortising the ends to receive the rail tenons
3. rounding the ends of the stiles

Referring to the technical drawing, lay out the dimensions of the rabbets. A router can be used to cut these, and it is done in two steps. First cut all the 1/4"-deep rabbets, then cut the 5/8"-deep rabbets. In order to ensure the same rabbett dimension on both stiles and the bottom rail, rout all three pieces before changing the depth of the router bit for the second set of rabbets.

Making the Top Rail

Lay out and cut the through rabbets using a table saw. Ensure that the dimensions arrived at with the stiles and bottom rail, are maintained on the top rail. Cut the 3/4"×3/4"×3" tenons on each end of the top rail. Also cut 3/4"×3/4"×2" tenons on either end of the bottom rail. Scribe a 24" radius curve on the top rail and cut it with a band saw. Sand it to final shape.

Making the Stiles

As shown in the technical drawing, mating mortises must be cut into the stile ends to receive the rail tenons. Cut 2 1/4" and 1 1/2" radii on the top and bottom ends respectively on the stiles.

Frame Assembly

Using a 1/4" roundover bit, round over the curved front inside edge of the top rail, and the front inside edge of the bottom rail. Dry assemble the frame. Mark where the rounded front inside edges meet the stiles. Round over the front inside edges of the stiles, stopping at the marks. After final asembly, the spots where the rounded inside edges of the stiles meet the rails can be blended to match.

Glue up and clamp the frame assembly. After the glue has dried, round over the outer front edge with a 1/2" roundover bit. Use a 1/4" roundover bit for the back outer edge of the frame.

Finishing

Since cherry is such a beautiful wood, I did not apply a stain. This allows the wood to age to its own soft, natural patina. Apply one coat of gloss polyurethane followed by two coats of satin polyurethane. Sand lightly between coats with 400-grit wet/dry paper, and wipe down the project after each sanding with a tack rag.

Final Assembly

After the finish has dried for at least 24 hours, assemble the mirror, the foamboard and the tempered hardboard to the frame. Screw the hardboard backing to the frame back. Since these screws hold the mirror assembly to the frame, plan to put a screw approximately every 4". Measure about 12" from the top rear of both stiles and mount the mirror-hanging plates. Attach the wire and hang your mirror.

Required Tools

Table or circular saw

Band saw or saber saw

Router

Sander

Drill

Tabletop Bookrack

This is a handy little rack for all the books you seem to need when doing a project, whether it's designing a piece of furniture or doing some writing. Made of cherry wood, stained with cherry stain and finished with a tung oil varnish, this rack will be a valued addition to your desk.

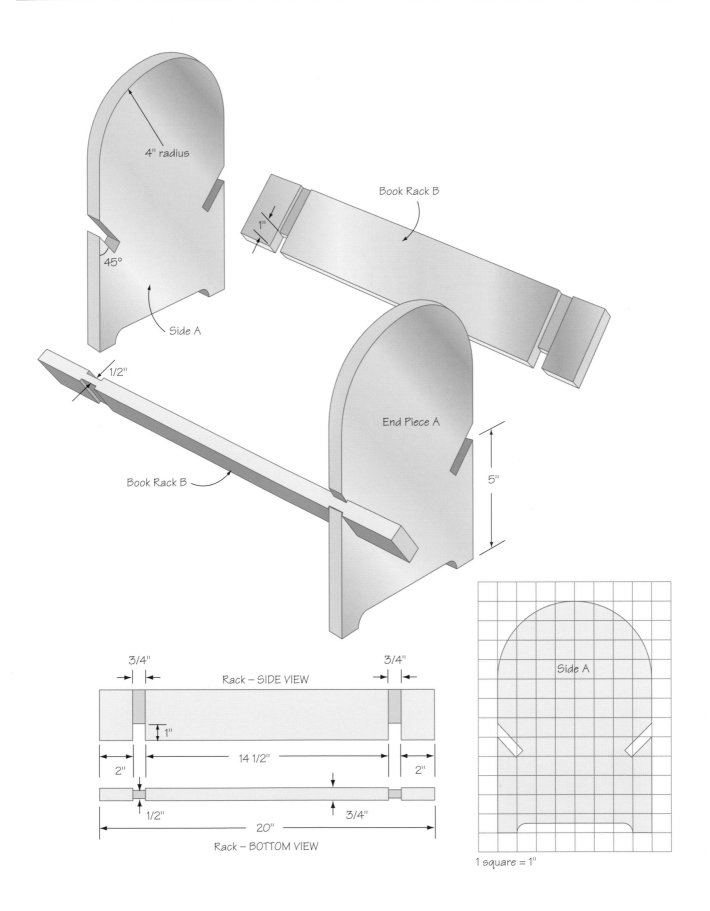

4" radius

45°

Side A

Book Rack B

1"

1/2"

Book Rack B

End Piece A

5"

3/4"

3/4"

Rack – SIDE VIEW

1"

14 1/2"

2"

2"

1/2"

3/4"

20"

Rack – BOTTOM VIEW

Side A

1 square = 1"

Cutting List • Tabletop Bookrack

REF.	QTY.	PART	STOCK	THICK	WIDTH	LENGTH	COMMENTS
A	2	End Pieces	¼ Cherry	¾	8	12	
B	2	Bookracks	¼ Cherry	¾	3	20	

Supplies

	Cherry Stain
	Tung Oil Varnish
	#600 Wet/Dry Paper

Making the End Pieces

Cut two 8"×12" blanks, and lay out all dimensions as shown in the technical drawing. Notice that the two rack slots are positioned 45° from the edge of each side. The 45° angle can be obtained by using a combination square. All cuts can be made by using either a band saw or a saber saw. Smooth all cuts and sand the flat surfaces. Rout a ¼" roundover on all outer edges.

Making the Bookracks

Size two ¼ boards to 3"×20" and layout the two slot dimensions on each board. Make a ¾" dado cut on each side approximately ⅛" deep so that a ½" center remains. The ¾" dimension has to fit the ¾" dimension on the end pieces. Using a band saw or saber saw, notch out two ¾"×1" slots as shown in the technical drawing. Check the fit between the book racks and the end pieces. Rout a ¼" roundover on all outer edges. Finish sand all surfaces.

Assembly

Final assembly consists of inserting both racks into the slots in the end pieces. Slight adjustments may be necessary. If made correctly, no gluing is necessary.

Finishing

Disassemble the project before applying the finish. I stained my bookrack with a cherry stain, and followed this with six coats of tung oil varnish. Between coats I sanded lightly with 600-grit wet/dry paper.

Indoor/Outdoor Table

This project can be made either as an indoor end table or as an outdoor side table. It all depends upon the wood that is used for its construction. For example: Outdoor use would dictate the use of a wood such as redwood or cedar, while for indoor use, a wood such as cherry would be appropriate. I have constructed this table both ways. The one described here was constructed of redwood. To add a little elegance to the project, two edges of each leg were slightly tapered. If desired, the legs can be left straight or turned. Either way is attractive. If the table is for outdoor use, a suitable water-resistant glue should be used.

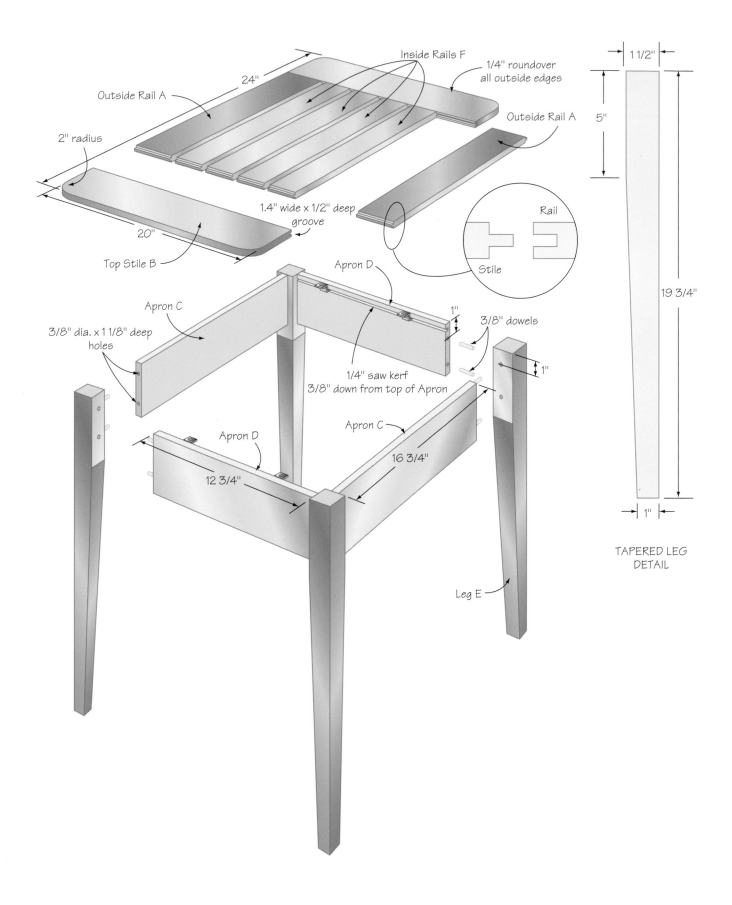

Inside Rails F

24"

Outside Rail A

1/4" roundover
all outside edges

Outside Rail A

2" radius

1 1/2"

5"

1.4" wide x 1/2" deep
groove

20"

Top Stile B

Rail

Stile

Apron D

Apron C

3/8" dia. x 1 1/8" deep
holes

1"

3/8" dowels

1/4" saw kerf
3/8" down from top of Apron

1"

19 3/4"

Apron D

Apron C

16 3/4"

12 3/4"

Leg E

1"

TAPERED LEG
DETAIL

Cutting List • Indoor/Outdoor Table

REF.	QTY.	PART	STOCK	THICK	WIDTH	LENGTH	COMMENTS
A	2	Outside Rails	Redwood	¾	3½	18	
B	2	Top Stiles	Redwood	¾	3½	20	
C	2	Side Aprons	Redwood	¾	4	16¾	
D	2	Front & Back Aprons	Redwood	¾	4	12¾	
E	4	Legs	Redwood	1½	1½	19¾	
F	4	Inside Rails	Redwood	¾	2½	18	

Hardware

	28	⅜"-Dia. x 1½" Dowels
	8	Fasteners (Woodcraft #27N10)

Supplies

	Carpenter's Glue (use waterproof glue if the table will be used outdoors)
	Seasonite (see Sources)
	CWF-UV (see Sources)

REQUIRED TOOLS

Table or circular saw

Jig saw, saber saw or band saw

Router

Tapering jig

Doweling jig

Dowel centers

Drill or drill press

Sander (or sandpaper and block)

Rails and Stiles

Cut all these parts to the dimensions listed in the bill of materials.

Making the Top Stiles

Either by using a router with a ¼" straight bit or by using a ¼" dado blade on the table saw, cut a ¼" × ½"-deep groove in both stiles as shown in the technical drawing (if a dado blade is not available, a regular blade can be used and the ¼" groove can be cut by making multiple passes). The stiles are made with a 2" radius. Make this cut with a saber saw or band saw and sand the edges smooth.

Making the Rails

All rails have ¼" tenons cut in them, sized to fit the groove in the stiles. Make sure there is a snug fit between the tenons and grooves.

Top Assembly

Dry assemble the top in order to determine the correct spacing of the inner rails. These were spaced .55" apart on the table that I built. This measurement can be obtained by using a vernier caliper similar to a 6" Stanley #35-019 dial caliper. After the correct positioning of the rails and stiles is determined, glue and clamp the entire assembly.

Aprons

Cut the aprons to the dimensions listed on the bill of materials. Cut a ¼"-deep saw-kerf on the back of each of the front and back aprons, ⅜" down from the top. This slot will be used during final assembly to secure the top to leg assembly. Lay out and bore two ⅜" holes in each end of the aprons to a depth of ¾".

Making the Legs

Cut the four 1½" square leg blanks to a length of 19¾". For reference, mark a 5" line around the four sides of each blank (this is where the slight taper will begin). As shown in the technical drawing, only two sides of each leg are to be tapered. At this time it's probably a good idea to mark all the inside edges of the legs. These are the sides to taper. Tapering can be done using the jig shown in Tools and Techniques.

The aprons are connected to the legs by ⅜" dowels. The dimensions of the ⅜" holes, previously bored in the apron ends, can be easily transferred to the legs by using a couple of ⅜" dowel centers and the simple doweling jig shown in Tools and Techniques. After these dimensions have been located in each leg, bore each hole with a ⅜" Forstner bit to a depth of ¾".

Leg and Apron Assembly

Before any gluing takes place, dry assemble the leg-apron assembly. Doing this now will point out any potential problems and preclude the need to unglue in order to fix the problem. Glue and press each of the dowels into the holes in the legs. Glue and clamp the respective two legs to the side aprons. After the glue has dried, glue the front and back aprons to the assembly. The squarness of the assembly can be checked by measuring the diagonal distance between legs. The two measurements should be about the same.

Final Assembly

Invert the top assembly on a bench, (bottom side up). Center the leg assembly on the top assembly. Insert the eight tabletop fasteners into the saw-kerfs, centering each one on an inside rail. Mark the location of the screw holes in each fastener. Drill eight pilot holes in the top assembly. Make sure you don't drill all the way through the top. Then screw the fasteners to the top.

Finishing

Since this table is to be used outdoors, I applied two coats of Seasonite (see Sources), allowing a minimum of four hours between coats. I waited at least six months after the second coat had dried and then applied two coats of CWF-UV (see Sources), wet-on-wet; that is, I applied the second coat as soon as the milkiness of the first coat disappeared. It is important not to allow any drying time between coats. Additionally, all end grain was given several wet-on-wet coats. This product can be applied every couple of years. It has the ability to restore the new look to redwood. One of the advantages of using these two products is that cleanup consists of washing the brushes with soap and water. There is no reason why this little table can't be put to use between the first and second steps.

Sources

Many of the projects in this book require the use of specific wood, hardware and finishing materials. There is nothing more frustrating than to need a part but not know where it can be obtained. So I have listed below the names and addresses of the companies where the required materials can be obtained.

HARDWARE

Rockler Woodworking and Hardware
4365 Willow Dr.
Medina, MN 55340
(800) 279-4441

Woodcraft
210 Wood County Industrial Park
P.O. Box 1686
Parkersburg, WV 26102-1686
(800) 225-1153, place an order
(800) 535-4482, customer service

WOOD

Memphis Hardwood Lumber Company
210 Church St.
P.O. Box 9
Memphis, NY 13112
(800) 286-3949

Woodcraft
210 Wood County Industrial Park
P.O. Box 1686
Parkersburg, WV 26102-1686
(800) 225-1153, place an order
(800) 535-4482, customer service

FINISHING

Old Masters
1900 Albany Place S.
P.O. Box 274
Orange City, IA 51041
(800) 747-3436

REDWOOD FINISHING PRODUCTS

The Flood Company
P.O. Box 399
Hudson, OH 44236-0399
(800) 321-3444

CHAIR TAPE

Shaker Workshops
P.O. Box 8001
Ashburnham, MA 01430-8001
(800) 840-9121

Index